LET'S ENJOY BIOCHEMISTRY QUIZ

700 UNIQUE MULTIPLE CHOICE QUESTIONS

SACHIN C NARWADIYA

ISBN 979-888591928-9

The book is dedicated to my dearest friend who encouraged me all the time whenever I was struggling for Education. She was my support like a base of a house. She was mine and always remain in me. The dedication also to my dear parents who brought up me for being a good citizen. I am dedicating my book to the persons living below poverty line and struggling daily on railway platforms, slums and much more places. We all know there is natur's rule playing for survival of fittest and some or other way weak will be flushed out of system. But as human being we need to take care of each other and live for each others walfare. I dedicate the book to Smt Lata Mangeshkar whose songs always inspired me for creative works.

Special dedication for costant support to me to my dearest wife Subha Narwadiya.

Contents

Foreword

Biological science is a vast subject of the science is necessary to the students going for medical or nonmedical field. This book is guideline for the students who are preparing for competitive exams with the subject of biological science. Give a chance to the students to understand the selection of answers of multiple-choice type of answer. Chapters of the book are covering the most of the basic and other studies of biological science.

This book is having different level of questions, Easy to very hard as prescribed for the competitive entrance exam. This book will enhance the knowledge of the students in the field of biological science. This book is handling over to the students with best wishes for their success.

Dr.Irfana Begum

Preface

The book is an useful tool for apirants of competetative examination. Those preparing for various competetions having biochemistry can solve the Questions. The questions were made in such a way that it will give readers enjoy of reading a book. It is opening of throught process of the readers. So lets enjoy reading solving questions. The questions were framed in such a way that will inclucate intrests and fill enthusiasm for Biochemistry.

Acknowledgements

The acknowledgement is a job of offering gratitude to those who came forwarding your support to do better. I acknowledge myrelatives, friends and office colleagues seniors for constant guidance and support. If I start writing names for anacknowledgement, it will be a long list that can cover many pages of the book. But still, I will have to offer my thanks to Dr Arvind C Ranade, Dr Mayuri Dutt, Dr Kalyani Panchbhai, Dr Shardul Wagh, Mrs Bharti Vaidya, Smt SubhaNarwadiya, Late Dr S K Dave, Mr Mithun Chakraborthy, Dr Sayed Shahzad, Fasiuddin Ahmed, Dr Imran Alam, Mr Prashant Sayre, Mrs Usha Chute, Mr Umesh Dhumne, Mr Nagesh Babu, Mr Nikhil Kulkarni, Mrs Shilpa Ingole, Dr Subroto Nandi, Dr Sarang Dhatrak,Dr Nakul Parashar, Mr Kapil Tripathi,Dr Bharat Bhushan,Dr Manish Mohan Gore,Dr Rakesh Upadhyay,Dr Abhishek Chauhan, DrIrfana Begum, ErAnujSinha, Mr Pradeep Kumar,Mr Ganesh Kalghuge,Mr Vipin Singh Rawat,Mr Ravindra,Mr Peeyush Nayyar,Mr Gagan Gupta,Mr Pawan Bhati also those supported me directly and indirectly. I acknowledge the pain taken and time devoted by Editor of this book Ms Vidhi Vashishtha for her valuable in-puts for upgradation of the book.

CHAPTER I

Medical Laboratory Biochemistry-01

1. Cell size is indicated by the terms normocytic, microcytic, and which of following options?

   A.Macrocytic B.Euglene C.Chromatic D. Normochromic
   2. How many substances are believed to be involved in the clotting process?

A. At least 10
B. At least 15
C. At least 20
D. At least 30

3. Partially activated coagulation factors are carried to the liver and the reticuloendothelial system, where what happened to them? A.They are segregated B.They are inactivated C.They are degraded D.They are reduced in numbers

   4. Prothrombin is a vitamin K−dependent protein produced by which organ? A.Liver B.Heart C.Muscles D.Bones
   5. Platelets survive in the circulation for about how many days? A.85 days B.25 days C.15 days D.10 days.
   6. Radial immunodiffusion allows measurement of the quantity of individual immunoglobulins to concentrations as low as which level out of following options?

A. 05 to 07 mg/dl
B. 30 to 40 mg/dl
C. 10 to 20 mg/dl
D. 40 to 50 mg/dl

7.

Bleeding time test may be performed using which method/s from following options?

A. Duke
B. Ivy
C. Template
D. All the above

8.

Cryoglobulin is an immunoglobulin that precipitates in those who develop high concentrations, causes the blockage of small capillaries in fingers, ears, and toes exposed to which temperatures?

A. normal temperatures
B. hot temperatures
C. cold temperatures
D. None of above

9.

The teichoic acid antibody is measured to diagnose infections caused by which bacterium?

A. *Staphylococcus aureus*
B. *Mycobacterium tuberculosis*
C. *Streptococcus*
D. *Escherichia coli*

10.

The euglobulin lysis time test is used to document which type of activity?

A. excessive fibrinolytic activity
B. reduced fibrinolytic activity
C. excessive erythropoiesis activity
D. reduced erythropoiesis activity

11.

All B lymphocytes have which of the following on their surfaces?

A. Immunoglobulin
B. Antigens
C. Heptane
D. Complement

12.

Hemoglobin content is indicated by the terms hypochromic,hyperchromic and one more from following options?

A. Microcytic
B. Macrocytic
C. Normochromic
D. Chromogenic

13.

Within a few months, through sequential suppression and activation of individual genes, Hgb F largely disappears and is replaced by adult hemoglobin having short form from following?

A. Hgb A
B. Hgb S
C. Hgb E
D. Hgb K

14.

Actual production of antibodies (immunoglobulins) occurs in plasma cells, the most differentiated form of which cells?

A. Basophils
B. Eosinophil
C. Neutrophils
D. B lymphocyte

15.

Diagnosis of Di George's syndrome, characterized by failure of which organ to develop, with a resulting decrease in T lymphocytes?

A. thymus
B. parathyroids
C. both A and B
D. none of above

16.

Diagnosis of X-linked agammaglobulinemia, characterized by severe deficiency of which cells?

A. Basophils
B. Eosinophil
C. Neutrophils
D. B lymphocyte

17.

Diagnosis of common variable hypogammaglobulinemia (CVH), characterized by absent, decreased, or defective B cells and most commonly caused by either lack of which of following?

A. helper T lymphocytes
B. abnormal suppressor T cells
C. both A and B
D. none of above

18.

The mixed lymphocyte culture (MLC) technique is widely used in testing before which of the following process?

A. Heart bypass surgery
B. Radiotherapy
C. Chemotherapy
D. Organ transplantation.

19.

Cryoglobulin can cause the blockage of which of following on exposed to cold temperatures?

A. small capillaries in fingers
B. ears and toes
C. Both A and B
D. None of above

20.

Which is/are the techniques can be used to assess Ig?

A. Serum protein electrophoresis
B. Immunoelectrophoresis and radial immunodiffusion
C. Radioimmunoassay
D. All the above

21.

The "alternate pathway" in complement activation bypasses which of following and begins directly with C3?

A. C1 activation
B. C4 activation
C. C2 activation
D. All the above

22.

The key step in the alternate pathway is activation of a serum protein without biologic effects in its inactive form, choose its name from following options?

A. Chymogen
B. Papain
C. Properdin
D. Biliverdin

23.

Method/s can be used to determine the circulating immune complexes (CIC) in the blood in the diagnosis of which of following condition/s?

A. Autoimmune diseases
B. Infectious diseases
C. Both A and B
D. None of above

24.

The radioallergosorbent test (RAST) for IgE measures the quantity of IgE antibodies in the serum after exposure to which of following?

A. General antibodies
B. Specific antibodies
C. Specific antigens
D. All the above

25.

Synovial fluid is a clear, pale yellow, and viscous liquid formed by secretion of a hyaluronate–protein complex by synovial cells is formed through which process?

A. Plasma ultrafiltration
B. Osmosis
C. Diffusion
D. Capillary actions

26.

Examination of synovial fluid for crystals is used in diagnosing for which disease?

A. Crystal-induced arthritis
B. Bone calcifications
C. Bone cancers
D. Rheumatic Fevers

27.

Phosphatidyl Glycerol appears in amniotic fluid at about how many weeks' gestation and indicates secretion of mature surfactant?

A. 18
B. 22
C. 26
D. 36

28.

Among the most common Hgb abnormalities are the sickle cell disorders, which exhibit which defect due to that result in the production of hemoglobin S (Hgb S)?

A. double beta- gene defect
B. double alpha-gene defect
C. HbF accumulation
D. HbA accumulation

29.

Sperm, which are in how much quantity of the volume of semen, are produced in the testis and mature in the epididymis?

A. less than 5 per cent
B. less than 3 per cent
C. more than 10 per cent
D. more than 15 per cent

30.

Which compound in semen is responsible for the fluorescence of semen in ultraviolet light, thus allowing detection of semen on clothing or other fabrics in rape cases?

A. Flavin
B. Fructose

C. Glucose
D. None of above

31.

Cholesterol crystals are associated with chronic joint effusions, which may be caused by which of following condition/s?

A. tuberculous arthritis
B. rheumatoid arthritis
C. Both A and B
D. None of above

32.

The Papanicolaou (Pap) smear is used primarily in the early detection of which disease?

A. Lung cancer
B. Prostate Cancer
C. Breast cancer
D. Cervical cancer

33.

The chemoreceptors are only able to sense dissolved oxygen molecules, not the oxygen that is bound to which of following?

A. Biliverdin
B. Bilirubin
C. Haemoglobin
D. Alveoli

34.

What is name of a chronic disorder that can occur in children or adults, and is characterized by the cessation of breathing during sleep?

A. Sleep apnea
B. Sleep dementia
C. Snoring
D. None of above

35.

How many molecules of ATPs are synthesized per NADH oxidation?

A. 2
B. 1
C. 3
D. 4

36.

Monosodium urate (MSU) crystals are associated with arthritis caused by which of following condition?

A. Hypertension
B. Diabetes
C. Cardio-vascular disease
D. Gout

37.

Why is the TCA cycle the central pathway of metabolism of the cell?

A. It occurs in the center of the cell

B. Its intermediates are commonly used by other metabolic reactions

C. All other metabolic pathways depend upon it

D. None of the above

38.

In what form does the product of glycolysis enter the TCA cycle?

A. AcetylCoA

B. Pyruvate

C. NADH

D. Glucose

39.

Malate-asparatate shuttle operates in

A. lungs and liver

B. heart and liver

C. pancreas and liver

D. none of these

40.

Which one is not the main protein in electron transport chain?

A. NADH dehydrogenase

B. Cytochrome bc1 complex

C. Cytochrome oxidase

D. Citrate synthease

41.

Polysaccharides on the surface of infecting microorganisms can also activate complement directly in the absence of

A. antibody via the alternative pathway

B. antigen via the alternative pathway

C. antibody via metabolic pathway

D. none of the above

42.

Antibodies bound to an invading microorganism activate the complement system via

A. classical pathway
B. metabolic pathway
C. Embden Meyerhof pathway
D. Entner-Doudoroff pathway

43.

The immune response to a booster vaccine is called a(n)
A. cellular response
B. innate response
C. primary response
D. secondary response

44.

Immunological memory is due to
A. short lived macrophage that can recognize specific pathogens
B. long lived B cells that secrete a specific antibody
C. long lived B cells that secrete a specific antigen
D. short lived helper T cells that signal macrophage to divide

45.

Bilirubin measurement in amniotic fluid is performed by spectrophotometric analysis, with the optical density (OD) of the fluid measured at wavelength intervals between which range.

A. 100 and 150 mm
B. 165 and 250 mm
C. 265 and 300 mm

D. 365 and 550 mm

46.

What is the result of an abnormal response of the immune system to part of a person's own body?
A. Passive immunity
B. Cancer
C. An allergic response
D. An autoimmune disease

47.

If a person is vaccinated against a disease sometime in the past, which of the following is currently in your body?
A. The disease organism itself and antigens for the disease organism
B. A very high level of antibodies against the disease antigens
C. Memory B lymphocytes for the antigen of this disease organism
D. All of the above

48.

Plasma cells produce thousands of _____________ that are released into the bloodstream
A. antigens
B. antibodies
C. helper T cells
D. virus fragments

49.

In cellular immunity, T lymphocytes are responsible for the recognition and killing of foreign invaders. The cells are
A. cytotoxic T lymphocytes (CTL)

B. killer T cells

C. both (a) and (b)

D. none of the above

50.

Which of the following immune cells would have an especially low count in a patient with advanced AIDS?

A. Killer T lymphocytes

B. Helper T lymphocyte

C. B lymphocytes

D. None of these

Answers

1.A	2.D	3.C	4.A	5.D	6.C	7.D	8.D	9.A	10.A
11.A	12.C	13.A	14.D	15.C	16.D	17.C	18.D	19.C	20.D
21.D	22.C	23.C	24.C	25.A	26.A	27.D	28.A	29.A	30.A
31.C	32.D	33.C	34.A	35.C	36.D	37.B	38.A	39.B	40.D
41.A	42.A	43.D	44.B	45.D	46.D	47.D	48.B	49.C	50.B

ANSWERS OF CHAPTER 1

CHAPTER II

Medical Laboratory Biochemistry-02

1.

Which report will often indicate whether a particular substance or group of substances is present without commenting on the complete composition of the sample?

A. Quantitative report
B. Qualitative report
C. Semi-Qualitative
D. None of Above

2.

Which of the following could be said to be a quantitative result?
A. The test is positive.
B. The sample contains more than 5 g of glucose.
C. The sample contains 0.3 g of glucose.
D. The sample contains both glucose and lactose.

3.

1 femtomol is equal to how many moles?
A. 10^{-10} moles
B. 10^{-12} moles
C. 10^{-15} moles
D. 10^{-18} moles

4.

Human Chorionic Gonadotropin (hCG) test is indicative for which of following?

A. Diabetes

B. Coronary Heart Disease

C. Arthritis

D. Pregnancy

5.

Hypernatremia word is used for patients with which condition?

A. Water Depletion

B. Increased blood volumes

C. Toxicants inhalation

D. None of above

6.

Hyponatremia is significant fall in which of following?

A. Serum Sodium

B. Serum Bilirubin

C. Serum Urobilinogen

D. None of above

7.

The effluent in column chromatography is which phase leaving the column?

A. mobile phase

B. stationary phase

C. ligand

D. None of above

8.

Luminol in an alkaline solution with hydrogen peroxide in the presence of iron or copper or an auxiliary oxidant produces which of following?

A. fluorescence

B. phosphorescence

C. chemiluminescence

D. None of above

9.

Which of following immunity is less specific and provides the first line of defense against infection?

A. Artificial Immunity

B. Innate Immunity

C. Acquired immunity

D. None of Above

10.

Interferon comprises a group of proteins produced by type of cells?

A. virus-infected cells

B. bacteria-infected cells

C. parasites-infected cells

D. None of above

11.

Complement, is a group of serum proteins that circulate in which state?

A. Active states

B. Separated

C. Sometimes active

D. Inactive state

12.

Which are common manifestations of immune dysfunction?

A. Allergy and asthma
B. Graft rejection and graft-versus-host disease
C. Autoimmune disease and Immunodeficiency
D. All the above

13.

Allergy and asthma are results of inappropriate immune responses, often to common antigens from which options given below?

A. plant pollen
B. food
C. animal dander
D. All the above

14.

The possibility that certain substances increased sensitivity rather than protection was recognized in about 1902 by Charles Richet, who attempted to immunize which animal against the toxins of a type of jellyfish, *Physalia*?

A. Goat
B. Dog
C. Rabbit
D. Monkey

15.

The physiologic barriers that contribute to innate immunity include

A. temperature
B. pH
C. various soluble and cell associated molecules
D. All the above

16.

Many species are not susceptible to certain diseases simply because...

A. Their normal body temperature inhibits growth of the pathogens
B. They have more numbers of antigens
C. They catch infection easily
D. None of above

17.

Chickens, for example, have innate immunity to anthrax because of which factor?

A. Their high body temperature
B. Their low body temperature
C. Their immunity is low
D. None of above

18.

A variety of soluble factors contribute to innate immunity are which of the following?

A. soluble proteins lysozyme
B. interferon
C. complement
D. all the above

19.

Lysozyme, a hydrolytic enzyme found in mucous secretions and in tears, is able to cleave which of the bacterial cell wall?

A. Peptin
B. Elastin
C. Peptidoglycan
D. None of above

20.

One of the principal mediators of the inflammatory response is histamine, a chemical released by which of the following?

A. Various phagosomes
B. Infecting Agents
C. Immunoglobulin
D. A variety of cells in response to tissue injury

21.

Adaptive immune responses exhibit which of following immunologic attributes:

A. specificity
B. diversity
C. memory and self/nonself recognition
D. all of above

22.

Transplantation of stem cell populations may be

A. autologous
B. syngeneic

C. allogeneic
D. all the above
23.

Of the body's normal 4 g of iron (somewhat less in women), how much percent resides in haemoglobin?

A. 30 percent
B. 65 percent
C. 20 percent
D. 3 percent
24.

Iron travels in the bloodstream bound to transferrin, a protein (beta-globulin) manufactured by which organ?

A. Liver
B. Heart
C. Kidney
D. Muscles
25.

Normally, only about 10 percent of ingested iron is absorbed, but up to 20 percent or more can be absorbed in cases of which condition from following options?

A. Leukaemia
B. Kidney damage
C. Iron deficiency anemia
D. Liver failure
26.

In humans, which vitamin from following options is obtained only by eating animal proteins, milk, and eggs?

A. vitamin B12
B. vitamin C
C. vitamin D
D. vitamin A

27.

Heme is composed of the red pigment porphyrin and iron,which is capable of combining loosely with which gas out of following?

A. carbon di oxide
B. hydrogen
C. nitrogen
D. oxygen

28.

Thalassemias are genetic disorders in globin chain synthesis that result in decreased production rates of -alpha and beta type of which protein chains?

A. Albumin chains
B. Globin chains
C. Keratin chains
D. None of above

29.

Normal erythrocytes rupture in saline solutions of 0.30 to 0.45 per cent. RBC rupture in solutions of greater than 0.50 per cent saline indicates which of following condition?

A. Increased fragility
B. Decreased fragility
C. Normal fragility
D. None of above

30.

The natural killer cell was first described in which year?

A. 1976
B. 1986
C. 1996
D. 1886

31.

The natural killer cell ,contains a small population of large, granular lymphocytes that display which type of activity against a wide range of tumor cells in the absence of any previous immunization with the tumor?

A. Lytic activity
B. Cytotoxic activity
C. Necrosis
D. None of above

32.

Haptens are small molecules that can bind to which of following options?

A. Cells
B. Antigens
C. Antibodies
D. None of above

33.

IgM accounts for 5%–10% of the total serum immunoglobulin, with an average serum concentration of which of following options?

A. 0.1 mg/ml
B. 0.5 mg/ml
C. 1 mg/ml
D. 1.5 mg/ml.

34.

Plasma makes up how much per cent of blood volume?

A. 25 to 30 percent
B. 35 to 40 percent
C. 45 to 60 percent
D. 85 to 90 percent

35.

Beginning at about age 5 years, the red marrow is gradually replaced by which coloured marrow, an inactive in the hematopoietic process?

A. Maroon
B. Black
C. Yellow
D. White

36.

The production rate of erythrocytes is at what rate from following options?

A. About 6 million cells per second
B. about 4 million cells per second

C. about 2 million cells per second

D. about 1 million cells per second

37.

People without kidneys or with severe impairment of renal function are unable to produce adequate amounts of renal erythropoietic factor. In these individuals, which organ became the source of erythropoietic factor?

A. Heart

B. Muscles

C. Liver

D. Bones

38.

Glucose-6-phosphate dehydrogenase is an enzyme pivotal in generating the reduced form of nicotinamide adenine dinucleotide phosphate (NADPH) through which pathway?

A. pentose pathway

B. metabolic mill

C. citric acid cycle

D. urea cycle

39.

Calcium plays an important role throughout the coagulation process.It is necessary for the activation of which factors from following?

A. VII

B. IX

C. X and XI

D. All the above

40.

Citrate, oxalate, and ethylenediaminetetra-acetic acid (EDTA) are anticoagulants because they bind which mineral and prevent it from participating in the clotting process?

A. Magnesium
B. Calcium
C. Iron
D. None of above

41.

When T3 and T4 hormones released in blood they binds to which of following?

A. Albumin
B. Globulin
C. Fructose
D. Mannose

42.

How much percentage of blood constitutes of total body weight?

A. 10 to 12 percent
B. 14 to 16 percent
C. 6 to 8 percent
D. 2 to 4 percent

43.

For how many days the platelets can survive in the circulation?

A. about 40 days
B. about 30 days
C. about 20 days
D. about 10 days.

44.

Two thirds of the total number of platelets is in the systemic circulation, and the remaining third exists as a pool of platelets in which organ?

A. spleen
B. liver
C. muscles
D. skin

45.

Disorders of platelet function (thrombopathies) are which of frequency of occurrence than disorders of platelet number?

A. less common
B. more common
C. similar
D. None of above

46.

If the platelet count falls below $10,000/mm^3$, what is effect on bleeding time?

A. Prolonged

B. Decreased

C. No effect

D. None of above

47.

Bleeding time is prolonged in von Willebrand's disease; an inherited deficiency of vWF associated with clotting factor VIII that is necessary for normal platelet adherence is actually belongs to which type from the following options?

A. a RNA

B. a gene

C. a protein

D. none of above

48.

Aspirin ingestion also prevents platelet aggregation and may prolong bleeding time for as long as how many days after a single 300-mg dose?

A. 15 days

B. 05 days

C. 10 days

D. 12 days

49.

Under the stress of anemia or hypoxia, an increased output of which of following options may lead to an increased number of circulating reticulocytes?

A. Erythropoietin

B. Erythrosine

C. Thrombin

D. Porphyrine

50.

Actual identification of which immunoglobin was accomplished by K. and T.Ishizaka in 1966?

A. IgD

B. IgE

C. IgG

D. IgA

1.B	2.C	3.C	4.D	5.A	6.A	7.A	8.C	9.B	10.A
11.D	12.D	13.D	14.B	15.D	16.A	17.A	18.D	19.C	20.D
21.D	22.D	23.B	24.A	25.C	26.A	27.D	28.B	29.A	30.A
31.B	32.B	33.D	34.C	35.C	36.C	37.C	38.A	39.D	40.B
41.A	42.C	43.D	44.A	45.A	46.A	47.C	48.B	49.A	50.B

ANSWERS OF CHAPTER 2

CHAPTER III

Human Physiology

1.

If glucose is not immediately metabolized, it can be stored in the liver or muscle in which form?

A. Lactose
B. Starch
C. Glycogen
D. Fructose

2.

Globulin levels show more variation than do albumin levels, probably because of which reason from below?

A. Single production site
B. Multiple production sites
C. It has different denaturation
D. None

3.

A low protein level and a reversed A-G ratio (i.e., decreased albumin and elevated globulins) suggest which disease?

A. Skin disorder
B. Heart Failure
C. Kidney Dysfunction
D. Chronic liver disease

4.

α1-Antitrypsin (α 1-AT) is an produced by the liver is which type of protein?

A. α 1-globulin
B. α 1- albumin
C. α 2-globulin
D. α 2- albumin

5.

Haptoglobin, an α 2-globulin which binds free hemoglobin released by the hemolysis of red blood cells in the bloodstream produced in which organ?

A. Liver
B. Kidneys
C. Spleen
D. Heart

6.

The three major types of body phospholipids are the lecithins, the cephalins, and which one more from following?

A. Glycerol
B. Sterols
C. Fatty acids
D. Sphingomyelins

7.

In the blood, the fat-soluble bilirubin binds to albumin as unconjugated (prehepatic) bilirubin for transport to which organ?

A. Liver
B. Kidneys
C. Spleen
D. Heart

8.

Most of the conjugated (posthepatic) bilirubin is excreted into the hepatic ducts and then into which of the following?

A. Liver
B. Bile
C. Plasma
D. Urine

9.

Phosphatases are enzymes that cleave phosphate from compounds with a single phosphate group. What is the optimum pH for its activity?

A. pH 9
B. pH 8
C. pH 12
D. pH 14

10.

Bone ALP predominates in normal serum, along with a modest amount of which options out of following?

A. RBC's enzymes
B. hepatic isoenzyme

C. renal enzymes

D. None

11.

Creatine phosphokinase (CPK), also called creatine kinase (CK), catalyzes the reversible exchange of phosphate between creatine and which of the following?

A. NADPH

B. AMP

C. ATP

D. ADP

12.

Creatine phosphokinase (CPK) exists almost exclusively in skeletal muscle, heart muscle, and, to a lesser extent, brain is important for which factor?

A. Important in intracellular storage

B. In release of energy

C. Both A and B

D. None

13.

Myoglobin is an oxygen-carrying protein normally found in cardiac and skeletal muscle. In acute myocardial infarction (AMI),myoglobin levels rise within how much time

A. 4 hour

B. 1 hour

C. 10 hour

D. 24 hour

14.

Renin is an enzyme released by the juxtaglomerular apparatus of the kidney in response to which of the following factor?

A. decreased extracellular fluid volume
B. decreased serum sodium
C. decreased renal perfusion pressure
D. All the above

15.

Drugs like anticoagulants, morphine, alcohol, salicylates in high doses, amphotericin-B, clofibrate, and certain anesthetics that may produce elevated level of which enzyme?

A. CPK
B. GGT
C. LDH
D. TSH

16.

Deficiencies in Growth Hormone are apparent only in which stage?

A. Childhood
B. Adulthood
C. Old ages
D. None

17.

Gastrin is secreted by the gastrin cells (G cells) of the gastric antrum, the pylorus, and the proximal duodenum in response to vagal stimulation and the presence of especially which type of food in the stomach?

A. Carbohydrates
B. Proteins
C. Fats
D. Vitamins
18.

Υ-Glutamyl transpeptidase (GGT),an isoenzyme of ALP, catalyzes the transfer of glutamyl groups among peptides and which of the following?

A. ketones
B. nitrogen
C. amino acids
D. None
19.

Alcohol, barbiturates, and phenytoin may elevate which of the following levels?

A. TSH
B. T3
C. T4
D. GGT
20.

Aspirin, adrenocorticosteroids, and heparin may produce which effect on TSH levels?

A. Increased TSH levels

B. decreased TSH levels
C. No Effect on TSH levels
D. None of above

21.

The hypothalamic–hypophyseal–gonadal axis can be evaluated by administering drugs and hormones known to affect specific hormonal interactions. These include which of the following?

A. Clomiphene
B. GnRH and hCG
C. Progesterone.
D. All the above

22.

Antidiuretic hormone (ADH) is formed by the hypothalamus but is stored which of the following gland?

A. In posterior pituitary gland
B. In anterior pituitary gland
C. In Thyroid gland
D. In Parathyroid gland

23.

The thyroid gland synthesizes its hormones from iodine and which essential amino acid ?

A. Threonine
B. Glycine
C. Tyrosine
D. Alanine

24.

The thyroid hormones thus formed are stored in the follicles of the gland bonded with which protein?

A. Albumin
B. Thyroglobulin
C. Globulin
D. Keratin

25.

About how much percent of cortisol is bound to cortisol-binding globulin (CBG) and albumin; the free portion is responsible for its physiological effects?

A. 20 percent
B. 50 percent
C. 90 percent
D. 70 percent

26.

Elevated cortisol levels occur in which disease having an excessive production of adrenocorticosteroids?

A. Sickle Cell Anaemia
B. Gullian Barr Syndrome
C. Cushing's syndrome
D. Myasthenia Gravis

27.

A diet high in amines (e.g., bananas, nuts, cereal grains, tea, coffee, cocoa, aged cheese, beer, ale, certain wines, avocados, and fava beans) may produce elevated which of the following?

A. plasma estrogen levels
B. plasma Progesterone levels
C. plasma TSH levels
D. plasma catecholamine levels

28.

Estrogens are secreted in large amounts by the ovaries and, during pregnancy, by which of the following options?

A. Stomach
B. Uterus
C. Kidneys
D. Placenta.

29.

Glucagon is secreted by the α cells of the islets of Langerhans in response to which of following parameter?

A. decreased blood glucose levels
B. increased blood glucose levels
C. increased cholesterol levels
D. decreased cholesterol levels

30.

The anion gap refers to the normal discrepancy between which of the following.

A. unmeasured cations in the blood
B. unmeasured anions in the blood
C. both A and B
D. None

31.

Which is the reservoir for calcium ions in human body?

A. Liver
B. Lungs
C. Kidneys
D. Bone

32.

Osmolality refers to the concentration of solutes in plasma or serum (particle number) or in which of the following options?

A. Urine (number of particles)
B. CSF (number of particles)
C. Bile (number of particles)
D. Respiratory Exudate

33.

What is the Normal Osmolality level range in Children which of the following?

A. 270–290 mOsm/kg
B. 350-400 mOsm/kg
C. 400-450 mOsm/kg
D. Below 100 mOsm/kg

34.

Arterial blood gas (ABG) determinations are made not only to determine levels of actual blood gases (i.e., oxygen and carbon dioxide) but also to assess the patient's which of the following parameter?

A. Minerals

B. Overall acid–base balance
C. Only Sodium level
D. Only Potassium level

35.

pO2 indicates the partial pressure of oxygen in the blood. When oxygen levels are lower than normal, the patient is said to be what?

A. Hyper
B. Hypoxic
C. Hypnotic
D. Metabolic Acidosis

36.

Vitamin A's precursor, carotene obtained from yellow or orange vegetables and fruits and from leafy green vegetables is which colour pigment?

A. Orange
B. Yellow
C. Blue
D. Green

37.

How many trace minerals are known to be essential to human function even though they are present in minute quantities in the body?

A. Six
B. Five
C. Seven
D. Eight

38.

pCO2 indicates the partial pressure of carbon dioxide in the blood, which is regulated by the which organ from following options?

A. Liver
B. Kidneys
C. Lungs
D. Gall Bladder

39.

These essential minerals are cobalt, copper, iodine, iron, manganese, molybdenum, and which one from following options?

A. Zinc
B. Sodium
C. Potassium
D. Mercury

40.

Which mineral is a constituent of vitamin B_{12} and is essential to the formation of red blood cells?

A. Cobalt
B. Iron
C. Sodium
D. Manganese

41.

Which mineral can functions as a coenzyme in urea formation and in the metabolism of proteins, fats, and carbohydrates?

A. Iron
B. Sodium
C. Manganese
D. Copper

42.

Presence of Biliverdin, Pseudomonas, Vitamins, Psychoactive drugs, Proprietary diuretics can be indicated by which colour of urine?

A. Yellow
B. Green
C. Blue
D. Balck

43.

The specific gravity of urine is an indication of the kidney's ability to reabsorb water and chemicals from which of the following options?

A. glomerular filtrate
B. blood entering in glomerulus
C. blood exiting from kidneys
D. None

44.

In abnormal conditions Blood can be present in the urine as which of the following options?

A. red blood cells
B. haemoglobin
C. Both A and B
D. None

45.

The major inherited disorders include phenylketonuria (PKU) the elevated levels of amino acids observed is which of the following?

A. Tyrosyluria
B. Alkaptonuria
C. Ornithine
D. Both A and B

46.

Elevated urinary copper levels are associated with which disease from the options given below?

A. Urea Stress
B. Wilson's disease
C. Uric Acid misbalance
D. None

47.

Which compound levels can also be elevated by excessive ingestion of strawberries, tomatoes, rhubarb, or spinach?

A. Malate
B. Melanine
C. Oxalate
D. Calcium

48.

Anabolic steroids (synthetic derivatives of testosterone) are used to enhance which of the following?

A. Mind Performance
B. Eyes Vision
C. Athletic performance
D. Breathing Capacity

49.

Cerebrospinal fluid (CSF) is secreted into the ventricles of the brain by specialized capillaries called as what?

A. Choroid plexuses
B. Hypothalamus
C. Grey Matter
D. None

50.

Although 500 to 800 ml of CSF is formed daily but how much amount are normally present?

A. 125 to 140 ml
B. 50 to 70 ml
C. 10-20 ml
D. 300-350 ml

1. C	2. B	3. D	4. A	5. A	6. D	7. A	8. B	9. A	10. B
11. C	12. C	13. B	14. D	15. A	16. A	17. B	18. C	19. D	20. A
21. D	22. A	23. C	24. B	25. C	26. C	27. D	28. D	29. A	30. C
31. D	32. A	33. A	34. B	35. B	36. B	37. C	38. C	39. A	40. A
41. C	42. B	43. A	44. C	45. D	46. B	47. C	48. C	49. A	50. A

ANSWERS OF CHAPTER 3

45

Toxicology

1.

Solanin toxicant is found in which of following options, can interferes in the transmission of nerve impulses?

A. Potato
B. Tomato
C. Grapes
D. Carrot

1.

A single molecule of ricin (shown, from castor seeds, LD50 = 2μg/kg) reaching the cytosol has been reported to kill which cell as a result of protein synthesis inhibition?

A. Tumour cells
B. Transposons
C. HeLa
D. P-cells

3.

Which term designates a rapid decrease in the response to a drug after repeated doses over a short period of time?

A. *Anayphylaxis*
B. *Tachyphylaxis*
C. *Hyphasis*
D. *Anophylaxis*

4.

Which term is used forinvestigation of the changes over time in the physiology and structure of an organism as a result of toxicant exposure?

A. *Toxicodynamics*
B. *Tachyphylaxis*
C. *Hyphasis*
D. *Anophylaxis*

5.

Which out of following is good example of Short time-frame: metabolic poisons?

A. Arsenic
B. Mercury
C. Halogens
D. Cyanide

6.

Northern analysis is usually used to identify and quantitate specifically which out of following in a sample?

A. mRNAs
B. tRNAs
C. rRNAs
D. none of above

7.

Which analysis is used to determine whether or not a gene of interest is present as well as its copy number?

A. Northern

B. Southern

C. Western

D. None of above

8.

In PCR it is necessary to know the flanking sequence of the DNA of interest in order to construct appropriate which of the options?

A. polymerase

B. pilots

C. primers

D. none of above

9.

Most of the recently developed methods for the detection, characterization, and quantitation of proteins (Leblanc, 2008) are immunoassays based on which fact?

A. Absence of metals in antigen and antibody reactions

B. Complement is required

C. Proteins are antigens, compounds that can be recognized by an antibody

D. None of above

10.

Western blotting is a widely used technique in which antibodies are used to detect proteins following electrophoresis, generally which polyacrylamide gel electrophoresis that permits the separation of proteins on the basis of their molecular weights?

A. sodium dodecyl sulfate

B. porous gel

C. agarose

D. agar

11.

Proteomics is represented by broad, inclusive techniques to separate, identify, and study the structure of the proteins of which of following?

A. hormones

B. enzymes

C. proteome

D. none of above

12.

In 1273, Edward I made the first which type of law, one that prohibited the burning of coal while Parliament was in session?

A. Anti-burning

B. antipollution

C. anti-corruption

D. none of above

13.

What is name of pollutants that come primarily from three sources: (1) combustion sources that burn fossil fuel for heating and power, or exhaust emissions from transportation vehicles that use gasoline or diesel fuels; (2) industrial processes; and (3) mining and drilling?

A. Anthropogenic Pollutants

B. Natural Pollutants

C. Man Made Pollutants

D. None of above

14.

Sulfur Oxides Sulfur dioxide is a common component of which of the following?

A. polluted air

B. polluted water

C. polluted ice

D. none of above

15.

Which of following can impair renal function, interfere with the development of red blood cells, and impair the nervous system, leading to mental retardation and even blindness?

A. Iron

B. Aluminium

C. Lead

D. None of above

16.

In case of rapid deprivation of body water death may occur how much decrease in water required?

A. 70%

B. 50%

C. 40%

D. 20%

17.

DNA or genomic libraries are collections of DNA fragments incorporated into a recombinant vector and transformed into which of the following?

A. appropriate host cell
B. suitable vector
C. bacteriophage
D. none of above

18.

Fushing of oil tankers plays a major role in which pollution?

A. riverine pollution
B. marine pollution
C. lake pollution
D. none of above

19.

Chronic high- level exposures of which option from following can cause abnormal skin pigmentation, hyperkeratosis, nasal congestion, and abdominal pain?

A. Arsenic
B. Iron
C. Aluminium
D. Lead

20.

In Japan in the 1950s and 1960s, wastes from a chemical and plastics plant containing mercury were discharged into which Bay?

A. Minamata Bay
B. Kyoto Bay
C. Tokyo Bay
D. None of above

21.

The most hazardous pesticides are the such as DDT (1,1,1 - trichloro - 2,2 - di(4 – chlorophenyl) ethane), aldrin, dieldrin, and chlordane they are which type of compunds?

A. organosulphure compounds
B. organocromate compounds
C. organochlorine compounds
D. organoarsenic compounds

22.

Persistent pesticides can accumulate in food chains; for example, shrimp and fish can concentrate some pesticides as much as how much folds?

A. 100–1000- fold
B. 10–100- fold
C. 1–10- fold
D. 1000–10,000- fold

23.

Nitrates from fertilizers leach readily from soils, and it has been estimated that up to how much % of applied nitrates enter water sources as runoff and leachate?

A. 40%
B. 50%

C. 60%

D. 70%

24.

Fertilizer phosphates, however, tend to be absorbed or bound to soil particles, so that only how much % of applied phosphates are leached into water?

A. 10-15%

B. 15-20%

C. 40-45%

D. 20 – 25%

25.

The increase in these nutrients, particularly which of following option, is of environmental concern because excess nutrients can lead to "algal blooms" or eutrophication, as it is known, in lakes, ponds, estuaries, and very slow moving rivers?

A. nitrate

B. potassium

C. acetate

D. phosphates

26.

When the dense algal growth dies, the subsequent biodegradation results in which conditions and the death of many aquatic organisms?

A. toxic conditions

B. anaerobic conditions

C. aerobic conditions

D. none of above

27.

There are two potential adverse health effects from nitrates in drinking water: nitrosamine formation and which one more from following?

A. Methemoglobinemia
B. Anaemia
C. Sickle cell anaemia
D. None of above

28.

The main organics that have been detected are chloroform, bromodichloromethane, dibromochloromethane, bromoform, carbon tetrachloride, and 1,2- d ichloroethane. These compounds are associated with an increased risk of which disese?

A. Blood Pressure
B. Fatigue
C. Hypoxia
D. Cancer

29.

Dioxins have contaminated large areas of which of following most notably with the extremely toxic TCDD (2,3,7,8 - tetrachlorodibenzo - p - dioxin) through industrial accidents and through widespread use of the herbicide 2,4,5- T.

A. water
B. soil

C. both A and B

D. none of above

30.

What is name given to airborne concentrations of substances and represent conditions under which it is believed that nearly all workers may be repeatedly exposed day after day without adverse effect?

A. Threshold limit values (TLVs)

B. Tertiary limit values(TLVs)

C. Secondary limit values (SLVs)

D. None of above

31.

Which values from following represent limits of amounts of substances (or their affects) to which the worker may be exposed without hazard to health or well-being as determined by measuring the worker ' s tissues, fluids, or exhaled breath?

A. Biologic limit values (BLVs)

B. Tertiary limit values(TLVs)

C. Secondary limit values (SLVs)

D. None of above

32.

The principal routes of industrial exposure are which of following?

A. dermal

B. inhalation

C. both A and B

D. none of above

33.

Cadmium is a cumulative toxicant with a biologic half-life of up to how many years in humans?

A. 30 years
B. 40 years
C. 50 years
D. 60 years

34.

More than 70% of the cadmium in the blood is bound to red blood cells; accumulation occurs mainly in the kidney and the liver, where cadmium is bound to which of following?

A. thyroglobulin
B. albumin
C. metallothionein
D. none of above

35.

Chromium toxicity results from compounds of hexavalent chromium that can be readily absorbed by the lung and gastrointestinal (GI) tract and, to a lesser extent, by which of following?

A. Genitals
B. Eyes
C. Skin
D. None

36.

Occupational exposure to which of following options may cause dermatitis, ulcers on the hands and arms, perforation of the nasal septum (probably caused by chromic acid), inflammation of the larynx and liver, and bronchitis?

A. Cr^{6+}
B. Na^+
C. NO_2
D. CO_2

37.

Chromate is a carcinogen causing bronchogenic carcinoma; the risk to chromate plant workers for lung cancer is how many times greater than that for the general population?

A. 50 times
B. 20 times
C. 40 times
D. 30 times

38.

Benzene affects the hematopoietic tissue in the bone marrow and also appears to be as which of following?

A. an immunosuppressant
B. an immunoenhancers
C. enzymes
D. none of above

39.

A major site of toxic action for metals is interaction with enzymes, resulting in which effect on the enzyme?

A. inhibition
B. activation
C. A and B both
D. None of above

40.

In the 19th century view by Arndt is that weak stimuli slightly accelerate vital activity, middle-strong stimuli raise it, strong ones suppress it and what is the effect of very strong stimuli?

A. Optimize it
B. Low down it
C. Accelerate it
D. Halt it

41.

Southam and Erlich, who reported the stimulatory effect of an antifungal when used at low doses, proposed which term?

A. Homisis
B. Hormesis
C. Candidiasis
D. None of above

42.

Low doses of cytostatic agents stimulate human Granulocytes and which one more cells growth out of following?

   A. Lymphocytes
   B. Eosinophil
   C. Neutrophil
   D. Basophils

43.

A single dose of an anti-tumoral immunosuppressive substance (cisplatin) is able to induce increased which activity?

   A. Natural killer cells activity
   B. Lymphokine-activated killer
   C. Eosinophil's activities
   D. None of above

44.

Low doses of toxicants awaken responses generally in which system?

   A. Digestive system
   B. Nervous System
   C. Immune system
   D. Circulatory system

45.

The Arndt-Schultz law says that every stimulus on a living cell produces an activity in what way proportional (within limits) to the intensity of the stimulus?

   A. Directly
   B. Inversely
   C. Adversely
   D. None of above

46.

Plants such as the black walnut, sycamore and sassafras trees release substances in the environment through their roots, leaves or by evaporation that limit the germination of competitors are termed as which type of plants?

A. Aromatic
B. Antipyric
C. Allelopathic
D. Nephrogenic

47.

Diclofenac is being replaced by another non-steroidal anti-inflammatory drug named as what?

A. Lysine
B. Methicillin
C. Cladomycine
D. Meloxicam

48.

Diclofenac was used to treat swelling and pain in cattle in India. As the drug became popular, the population of vultures decreased by 95 %, as the vultures eating cattle carcasses died of which disease?

A. Lungs Failure
B. Heart failure
C. Kidney failure
D. None of above

49.

What is the term used for the regurgitation of a poison taken via the oral route?

A. Poisoned
B. Emesis
C. Analysis
D. Estimate

50.

Intoxication is dealt with by which of the following method/methods?

A. Treatment with an antidote, antagonist, metabolic modulator or substrate
B. Allowing the body's own regenerative powers to take over
C. Removal of toxicants
D. All the above

1. A	2. C	3. B	4. A	5. D	6. A	7. B	8. C	9. C	10. A
11. C	12. B	13. A	14. A	15. C	16. D	17. A	18. B	19. A	20. A
21. C	22. D	23. A	24. D	25. D	26. B	27. A	28. D	29. C	30. A
31. A	32. C	33. A	34. C	35. C	36. A	37. B	38. A	39. C	40. D
41. B	42. A	43. B	44. C	45. B	46. C	47. D	48. C	49. B	50. D

ANSWERS OF CHAPTER 4

CHAPTER V

Bioinformatics and Biophysical Techniques

1.

The instrument which is used to study the absorption or emission of radiation as function of wavelengths is called as what?

A. pH meter
B. Spectrophotometer
C. Anemometer
D. Hydrometer

2.

What is name of instrument used to resolve polychromatic radiations into its individual wavelengths?

A. Monochromators
B. Slit
C. Chrome
D. Lens

3.

Standard Wavelength of a cuvette is which of following?

A. 1 meter
B. 1 cm
C. 1 mm
D. 1 nm

4.

Photocells, Phototubes and photomultiplier tubes are which type of instruments?

A. Activators
B. Atomizers
C. Detectors
D. Enhancers

5.

What is name of phenomenon of absorbing radiations and emitting into longer wavelengths?

A. Refraction
B. Reflections
C. Emission
D. Fluorescence

6.

What is name of a shift when a material absorbs in ultraviolet region and emits into visible region?

A. Beer Lambert
B. Stoke's
C. H-H Equation
D. Enzyme Kinetics

7.

In general, at which temperature range the Fluorescence is maximum?

A. 55-65°C
B. 25-30 $^\circ$C

C.   45-50°C

D.   70-75°C

8.

Xenon arc can be used as which of the following?

A.   Continuous source of radiation

B.   An absorptive device

C.   Dark body

D.   Coloured absorber

9.

Which are the key features for identifying proteins from options given below?

A.   their electrical charge

B.   their molecular mass

C.   Both A and B

D.   None of above

10.

The history of Liquid Chromatography (LC) began at

A.   early 20th century

B.   early 18th century

C.   end of 18th century

D.   None of above

11.

The light microscope has come a long way since Hans and Zacharias Janssen created the first 'compound' microscope in which year?

A. 1190
B. 1390
C. 1490
D. 1590

12.

The unaided human eye can resolve two points as close as how much apart?

A. 250 mm apart
B. 50 mm apart
C. 100 mm apart
D. 150 mm apart

13.

The wavelength range of visible light and the numerical aperture of microscope lenses together combine to constrain the maximum theoretical resolution of the light microscope to which of the following value, irrespective of maximum magnification?

A. 0.44 mm
B. 0.33 mm
C. 0.22 mm
D. 0.11 mm

14.

Kohler illumination, introduced early last century by August Kohler, has become the universally used because of the quality of image produced is of which form?

A. Bright Field illumination
B. Dark field illumination

C. Fluorescence Illumination

D. None of Above

15.

Fluorescence microscopy takes advantage of the property of molecules called fluorochromes to emit light of a particular wavelength when excited by incident light of which wavelength from the options below?

A. Shorter

B. Longer

C. Medium

D. Same

16.

The BACTEC 9000 series (9240, 9120, 9050) of blood culture instruments (Becton Dickinson) are designed for the rapid detection of which of following?

A. Minerals in clinical specimens

B. Microorganisms in clinical specimens

C. Blood in clinical specimens

D. None of Above

17.

Reverse transcription polymerase chain reaction (RT-PCR) commonly detects mRNA but also detects to which of following target unless steps are taken to destroy this target? (Dilworth & McCarrey, 1992).

A. Proteins

B. DNA

C. Ribosomes

D. None of Above

18.

Lead carbonate was used for which work in Rome?

A. as a contraceptive
B. as a pain killer
C. as an anti-bacterial
D. None of above

19.

Use of VIS and UV/VIS spectrophotometers in water analysis began in which year?

A. 1940s
B. 1900s
C. 1990s
D. 2010s

20.

the Coleman universal spectrophotometer was used in water laboratories for analysis of iron, manages, phosphate, silicate, and sulphate in the which range of spectrum?(Müller, 1954)

A. Infrared
B. Visible
C. Ultraviolet
D. None of above

21.

The Beckman DU spectrophotometer, the first commercial field instrument of its type for water analysis in the UV–VIS spectra, was introduced in which year?

A. 1300
B. 1941
C. 1890
D. 1972

22.

It was Isaac Newton who discovered that white light was a mixture of colours that could be separated into its components using which of following?

A. Magnifying Glasses
B. Lenses
C. Monochromator
D. Prism.

23.

By the 1800s, the world was ready for precision measurements of wavelength, and the birth of which of following occurred?

A. Reading through lenses
B. Photometry
C. Quantitative spectroscopy
D. Microscopy

24.

The first automated, recording spectrophotometer was developed between 1926 and 1928 by which scientists at the Massachusetts Institute of Technology?

A. J Thomas

B. Henry Becquerel
C. Hardy and his colleagues
D. None of Above

25.

A microsatellite locus typically has tens of alleles (copy numbers of repeating unit), which can be determined via which techniques from unique flanking sequences?

A. Southern Blot
B. ELISA
C. Microarrays
D. PCR amplification

26.

Statistics is a branch of which subject that targets on the collection, organization, and interpretation of numerical data, especially on the analysis of population characteristics by inferences from random sampling?

A. Bioinformatics
B. Biology
C. Mathematics
D. Physics

27.

Computational prediction of gene boundaries and noncoding exons is extremely difficult because most predictions have been focusing on which regions?

A. coding regions
B. non- coding regions
C. silence regions

D.   None of above

28.

Two common strategies have been used in ab initio gene prediction algorithms: (a) detecting individual exon candidates and connecting them by, e.g., Dynamic Programming (DP) and (b) segmenting DNA sequence into exon/intron/splice-site states by (standard or generalized) which models from following options?

A.   3 D protein models
B.   2 D protein models
C.   Population Genetic Models
D.   Hidden Markov models

29.

Recent experimental advance (50RACE, CAGE-tag sequencing, PolII (or PIC, or H3K4me3) ChIP-chip or ChIP-Seq, etc.) has produced genome-wide mapping of mammalian core-promoter/TSS data for which of following options?

A.   Some Plasmids
B.   Some tumours
C.   Few tissue cultures
D.   Few cell lines.

30.

A pH meter basically works on measurement of which factor?

A.   Voltage differences
B.   Movement

C. Evaporation

D. None of above

31.

A dynamic programming method similar to those explained was first introduced for which type of sequence alignment by Needleman and Wunsch and Smith and Waterman?

A. Pair-wise

B. Unpaired

C. Unmatched

D. None of above

32.

The machine is used for working in place of heart during the bypass surgery is termed by which name?

A. Heart-Lung Machine

B. Heart-Liver Machine

C. Spirometer

D. None of above

33.

The principle of flame photometer is based on the measurement of the emitted light intensity when which of following option is introduced into the flame?

A. a metal

B. a chemical

C. a gas

D. a non-metal

34.

Chromatographic techniques can be classified into how many main categories based on the type of molecular interactions used for separation?

A. Four
B. Five
C. Six
D. Seven

35.

Separation by affinity chromatography is based on a biological property of macromolecules rather than on which property out of following?

A. physical property
B. chemical property
C. specific gravity
D. none of above

36.

When zone electrophoresis is combined with molecular exclusion effects using gels, than what can be achieved?

A. much higher resolutions
B. much lower resolutions
C. medium resolutions
D. no resolutions

37.

Isoelectric focussing is an electrophoretic method where which gradient is used along with the voltage gradient?

A. Ice cooled
B. Volume
C. pH
D. Gravity

38.

In continuous flow electrophoresis the experiment is conducted in free solution without which of following options?

A. Gel
B. Buffer
C. pH
D. Supporting medium

39.

The sedimentation of a suspension of particles in a liquid can be achieved either by the force of gravity or by an applied which type of force?

A. centrifugal force
B. centripetal force
C. elliptical force
D. None of above

40.

Ultracentrifuge The sample is held in a centrifugal cell in which type of rotor, which is rotated by an electric motor at speeds up to 70,000 revolutions per minute (rpm)?

A. titanium
B. aluminium
C. Both A or B

D. None of above

41.

Viscosity is resistance to which of following property?

A. To become thick
B. crystallization
C. liquid flow
D. cooled to ice

42.

Molecules in solution undergo both translational and rotational displacements due to which effect of the solvent?

A. Buffer action
B. Beer-Lambert
C. Tyndall
D. Brownian motion

43.

Light scattering is a technique widely used to determine which factor of macromolecules in solution?

A. molecular intensity
B. molecular affinity
C. molecular weight
D. molecular vicinity

44.

Small Angle X-ray Scattering this technique is analogous to that of which technique?

A. Light reflection

B. Light refraction

C. Light absorption

D. Light scattering

45.

Most biological molecules or systems are optically active; i.e. they rotate the plane of polarised light. If the rotation is clockwise of the light source and if the rotation is counter clockwise than they are known as what?

A. dextro-rotatory and levo-rotatory

B. levo-rotatory and dextro-rotatory

C. both A and B

D. none of above

46.

Infrared radiation is heat radiation and term 'infrared' extends from which range on the electromagnetic spectrum?

A. 10^{12} to 10^{10} Hz

B. 10^{11} to 10^{10} Hz

C. 10^{14} to 10^{10} Hz

D. 10^{13} to 10^{10} Hz

47.

The Raman effect was discovered by C.V. Raman and his associates in which year?

A. 1965

B. 1886

C. 1900

D. 1928

48.

The wavelength of the electron beam depends on its energy, which is in turn dependent on which of following used to accelerate the electrons?

A. Voltage
B. Current
C. Resistance
D. None of above

49.

Modern electron microscopes use accelerating voltages in which range?

A. 1000 volts to 1000 kilovolts.
B. 100 volts to 100 kilovolts.
C. 10 volts to 100 kilovolts.
D. 1 volts to 10 kilovolts.

50.

According to the de Broglie equation, this voltage will correspond to a wavelength of about how much of angstrom?

A. 0.03 Å.
B. 0.01 Å.
C. 0.02 Å.
D. 0.04 Å.

1. B	2. A	3. B	4. C	5. D	6. B	7. B	8. A	9. C	10. A
11. D	12. D	13. C	14. A	15. A	16. B	17. B	18. A	19. A	20. B
21. B	22. D	23. C	24. C	25. D	26. C	27. A	28. D	29. D	30. A
31. A	32. A	33. A	34. A	35. A	36. A	37. C	38. D	39. A	40. C
41. C	42. D	43. C	44. D	45. A	46. C	47. D	48. A	49. A	50. A

ANSWERS OF CHAPTER 5

Clinical and Nutritional Biochemistry

1.

Except which amino acid, all amino acids have asymmetric (chiral) carbon so they are optically active?

A. Glycine
B. Alanine
C. Serine
D. Threonin

2.

Which type of amino acids represents the vast majority of amino acids found in proteins?

A. L-amino acids
B. D-amino acids
C. Both equally
D. None of above

3.

Which amino acids are found in some proteins produced by exotic sea-dwelling organisms, components of the peptidoglycan cell walls of bacteria?

A. L-amino acids
B. D-amino acids
C. Both equally
D. None of above

4.

Amino acids are classified as basic, acidic, aromatic, aliphatic, or sulfur-containing based on the properties of which group?

A. their CO group
B. their O group
C. their NH group
D. their R groups
5.

Which type of malnutrition is the most widespread form of malnutrition among pre-school children of our country?

A. Protein Energy Malnutrition
B. Carbohydrates Malnutrition
C. Fats Malnutrition
D. None of above
6.

Nutritional blindness which affects over seven million children in India per year results mainly from the deficiency of which vitamin, coupled with protein energy malnutrition?

A. Vitamin C
B. Vitamin A
C. Vitamin D
D. Vitamin K
7.

Choose odd one from following in case of under-nutrition resulting in which conditions?

A. Protein Energy Malnutrition (PEM)
B. Iron deficiency
C. Obesity
D. Iodine deficiency

8.

A radionuclide (radioactive nuclide) is a nuclide with which type of nucleus?

A. balanced and stable
B. unbalanced and unstable
C. non active
D. none of above

9.

What is the term used for the any substance which is capable of inhibiting, retarding or arresting the growth of micro-organisms, or any deterioration of food due to micro-organisms, or of making the effect evidence of any such deterioration?

A. Toxicants
B. Enantiomers
C. Enhancers
D. Preservative

10.

The single Lethal Dose that kills 50 % of animals (LD_{50}) has historically been the landmark for which purposes out of following?

A. Morbidity
B. Death Rate

C. Toxic levels
D. Classification
11.

Milder cases of Vitamin C Deficiency associated with which symptoms?

A. Fatigue
B. Irritability
C. Increased severity of respiratory tract infections
D. All the above
12.

Most animals make large amounts of vitamin C, converting glucose to ascorbate in how many enzymatic steps?

A. Four
B. Three
C. Two
D. One
13.

In the course of evolution, humans and some other animals—gorillas, guinea pigs, and fruit bats—have lost the last enzyme in converting glucose to ascorbate and now they obtain ascorbate in what?

A. Diet
B. Blood
C. Liver
D. Air
14.

According to 2008 Guinness World Records, thaumatin (also known as talin) is the sweetest known substance. It is how many times as sweet as sucrose?

A. 1,600 times
B. 1,100 times
C. 600 times
D. 200 times

15.

In East Asia, where polished white rice was the common staple food of the middle class, which disease resulting from lack of vitamin B1 was endemic?

A. Pellagra
B. Beriberi
C. Kwashiorkor
D. Goitre

16.

The gastrointestinal tract constitutes the process of digestion and involves enzymes. The majority of the enzymes involved in the digestive process are of which type?

A. Reductase
B. Oxidase
C. Lipase
D. Hydrolases

17.

One constituent of human saliva is amylase which catalyses the hydrolysis of starch. Approximately how much litres of saliva is secreted daily?

A. 0.75 L
B. 1 L
C. 1.5 L
D. 2.0 L

18.

From the mouth the food contents pass via the esophagus to the stomach where they come in contact with gastric juice at which pH?

A. pH equal or less than 11
B. pH equal or less than 5
C. pH more than 6
D. pH equal or less than 2

19.

The alkaline content of pancreatic (about 1.5 L/day) and biliary secretions (0.5 L/day) neutralize the acid of the chyme and change the pH to the alkaline side necessary for the optimum activity of which enzymes?

A. Pancreatic
B. Intestinal
C. Both A and B
D. None of above

20.

The digestion of starch begins in which organ?

A. liver
B. intestine

C. stomach

D. mouth

21.

Fat constitutes about how much % of dietary lipids and provides energy in a highly concentrated form?

A. 40%

B. 60%

C. 90%

D. 70%

22.

Colipase, which binds to both the water-lipid interface and to lipase, thereby anchoring and activating the enzyme, what is the molecular weight of colipase?

A. 20,000

B. 10,000

C. 30,000

D. 40,000

23.

Colipase is secreted by the pancreas as pro-colipase (inactive) simultaneously with lipase in which ratio?

A. 1:3 ratio

B. 1:4 ratio

C. 1:2 ratio

D. 1:1 ratio

24.

The proteolytic enzymes are synthesized in which cells of the pancreas and secreted in pancreatic juice as zymogens?

A. acinar cells
B. actin cells
C. beta cells
D. none of above

25.

In lactase deficient patients lactose gets accumulated which is a good energy source for microorganisms in the colon, and they ferment it to lactic acid and generate which of the following compounds?

A. Methane (CH_4)
B. Hydrogen gas (H_2)
C. Both A and B
D. None of above

26.

PKU is an autosomal recessive metabolic genetic disorder characterized by a deficiency in the enzyme phenylalanine hydroxylase (PAH), of which organ?

A. Hepatic
B. Intestine
C. Heart
D. Lungs

27.

What is name of a rare genetic metabolic disorder that affects an individual's ability to metabolize the sugar galactose properly?

A. Hypothyroidism
B. Hypoglycaemia
C. Galactosemia
D. Ketouria

28.

Which are the most common cow milk allergens?

A. Casein fractions
B. β-lactoglobulins (β-lg)
C. Both A and B
D. None of above

29.

As per estimation the production of 1 liter of milk requires how much litres of blood moving through the mammary gland to provide the milk precursors?

A. 100 liter
B. 300 liter
C. 400 liter
D. 500 liter

30.

Cow's milk contains how much percentage of fat?

A. 1.5 to 3%
B. 3.5 to 5%
C. 2.5 to 3%
D. 2.5 to 4%

31.

The site of lactose synthesis is the membranes of which cell organelle?

A. ER
B. Cytoplasm
C. Mitochondria
D. Golgi apparatus

32.

The project Integrated Child Development Services (ICDS) was launched in which year?

A. 1960
B. 1950
C. 1975
D. 1989

33.

What is common among BHA (Butylated hydroxyl anisole), BHT (Butylated hydroxyl toluene), PG (propyl gallate) and TBHQ (Tertiary butyl hydroquinone) ?

A. All are esters
B. All are ketones
C. All are acidic
D. All phenolic

34.

Many metals exist in food in a naturally chelated form, such as, Mg in chlorophylls, Fe in ferreitin and hemoglobin and Cu, Zn and Mn in which of the following options?

A. Proteasomes
B. Transmitters
C. Enzymes
D. Hormones

35.

One of the best known, most widely used and somewhat controversial flavors enhancer is monosodium glutamate (MSG), the sodium salt of the naturally occurring which of following?

A. Glutamic acid
B. Galactose
C. Glucose
D. Fructose

36.

Human beings cannot synthesize vitamin C and hence require it in their diet, what is the daily requirement is of this vitamin?

A. 30 mg
B. 60 mg
C. 80 mg
D. 40 mg

37.

Fermented foods can be divided into how many goups?

A. Eighth groups
B. Seven groups
C. Nine groups
D. Ten groups

38.

The cooler regions of Europe, Scandinavia, Poland and Russia will produce and consume beers and lagers from which of following?

A. Grapes
B. Sugar can
C. Rice
D. Barley

39.

Distillation will increase the alcohol strength and produce spirits of many types, e.g. whisky, brandy, vodka, gin, rum, etc., which can contain between which range of ethanol percentages?

A. 10 and 20% ethanol
B. 20 and 30% ethanol
C. 30 and 35% ethanol
D. 40 and 50% ethanol

40.

The southern warmer climate of Spain, Greece, Italy and France will have much higher production and consumption of wines derived from which of the following crop?

A. Grapes
B. Sugar can
C. Rice
D. Barley

41.

Saccharomyces cerevisiae has a high tolerance to which of following?

A. Acetone
B. Acids
C. Water
D. Ethanol

42. Which was the first eukaryote to have its complete genome sequenced?

A. *Saccharomyces cerevisiae*
B. Moulds
C. Grass hoper
D. Rabbits

43. Historically, wine is which type of drink out of following?

A. European drink
B. Asian drink
C. American drink
D. African drink

44. Most commercial wines use the wine grape named as what?

A. *Vitis vinifera*
B. Nasik Grapes
C. Smaller grapes

D. None of above

45.

Red wine is formed when which grapes are crushed and fermented whole?

A. Black
B. Green
C. Yellow
D. Blue

46.

If the skins are removed from black grapes or when white grapes are used , which colour wine is the final product?

A. Green
B. Blue
C. Red
D. White

47.

Fermentation conditions such as time and temperature will depend on which option from following?

A. Concentration of wine desired
B. Quantity of wine desired
C. Type of wine desired
D. None of above

48.

Modern scientific research now supports the view that moderate wine consumption is associated with which of following options?

A. lower coronary heart disease mortality
B. lower diabetes disease mortality
C. lower thyroid disease mortality
D. lower communicable disease mortality

49.

Fortified wines, such as sherry, port and vermouth, are wines to which additional alcohol is added after fermentation, raising the alcohol level to about how much percentage?

A. 13%
B. 10%
C. 5 %
D. 20%

50.

Whisky has been produced in Scotland for hundreds of years and is a continuing biotechnology success story. It is known as which of the option?

A. 'Water of Thirst'
B. 'Water of Death'
C. 'Water of Life'
D. None of above

1. A	2. A	3. B	4. D	5. A	6. C	7. C	8. B	9. D	10. D
11. D	12. A	13. A	14. A	15. B	16. D	17. C	18. D	19. C	20. D
21. C	22. B	23. D	24. B	25. C	26. A	27. C	28. C	29. D	30. B
31. D	32. C	33. D	34. C	35. A	36. D	37. C	38. D	39. D	40. A
41. D	42. A	43. A	44. A	45. A	46. D	47. C	48. A	49. D	50. C

ANSWERS OF CHAPTER 6

CHAPTER VII

Biotechnology

1.

Traditional biotechnology refers to the conventional techniques that have been used for many centuries to produce which of the following?

A. Beer
B. Wine
C. cheese
D. All the above

2.

'New' biotechnology embraces which methods of genetic modification by recombinant DNA and cell fusion techniques together with the modern developments of 'traditional' biotechnological processes?

A. Some methods of genetic modification
B. All methods of genetic modification
C. Only selective methods of genetic modification
D. None of Above

3.

In truth, genetic modification has been used by mankind for over 10000 years to improve plants and animals by which of the following options?

A. selective breeding

B. differential breeding

C. cross breeding

D. none of abobe

4.

It was the discovery of antibiotics in 1929 and their subsequent large-scale production in the 1940s that created the greatest advances in which technology?

A. Fermentation technology

B. Genetics

C. Recombinant DNA Techniques

D. Cell lines and cell cultures

5.

Prior to 1982, insulin for diabetics was derived from which animal's pancreases?

A. Rabbit and Monkeys

B. Goat and Ship

C. Mice and Rat

D. Beef and Pork

6.

Biotechnology may well make it possible to economically produce orphan drugs, here what is meaning of orphan drugs?

A. Drugs with high potency

B. Drugs with low potency

C. Drugs with less side effects

D. Drugs with specific needs and small profit return

7.

Recombinant blood factors used for the disease Haemophilia A is which of the following?

A. Factor VIII
B. Factor V
C. Factor VI
D. Factor IV

8.

Recombinant growth factors erythropoietin is indicative for which disease?

A. Cardiovascular Diseases
B. Cataract
C. Anaemia
D. Diabetes

9.

Herceptin, ProtaScint are examples for which option from following developed for Breast cancer, prostate adenocarcinoma?

A. Antigens
B. Monoclonal antibodies
C. Attenuated Vaccines
D. None of above

10.

The DNA sequences coding for the therapeutic proteins can also be modified by direct mutagenesis allowing further changes in protein structure. This is called protein engineering and the mutated proteins are termed as what?

A. Mutants
B. Metantss
C. Muteins
D. None of above

11.

The growth hormone, somatostatin, has been extremely difficult to isolate from animals; half a million sheep brains were required to extract how much quantity of pure somatostatin?

A. 0.50g
B. 0.5g
C. 0.05g
D. 0.005 g

12.

What the rate in children suffering from hypopituitary dwarfism resulting from growth hormone deficiency ?

A. One child in 5000
B. One child in 50000
C. One child in 500000
D. One child in 5000000

13.

In 1957, two British researchers discovered substances produced within the body that could act against viruses by making cells resistant to virus attack. What is name of that substance?

A. Interleukin
B. Interferon

   C. Cytoplasmin

   D. Plastids

14.

Human interferons believed to play a part in controlling many types of viral infections, including the common cold, as well as having potential in controlling cancer are of which nature?

   A. Co factors

   B. Minerals

   C. Steroids

   D. Glycoproteins

15.

Interferon produced by Rats is having which effect for virus infecting human beings?

   A. Not effective

   B. May some time effective

   C. Very Effective

   D. None

16.

There are many different types of interferons characteristic of what?

   A. individual species of animals

   B. individual species of plants

   C. individual species of bacteria

   D. None of above

17.

Most early human interferon production was carried out in which country?

A. Finland
B. Japan
C. Rome
D. USA

18.

Most early human interferon production was executed by using which cells?

A. Leucocytes from blood
B. Epithelial cells
C. Spores
D. Bacterial Cells

19.

Two sources of interferon are currently available. The first is from human diploid fibroblasts growing attached to a suitable surface and the interferon produced is widely considered to be the safest available. The second source is from which of following?

A. Viruses
B. Bacteria
C. Yeast
D. Parasites

20.

Lymphokines are proteins produced by which of the following?

A. Eosinophil
B. Monocytes
C. Lymphocytes
D. Fibroblasts

21.

Recombinant erythropoietin is used therapeutically mainly in which disease treatment also it was the first recombinant therapeutic protein to achieve US$1 billion sales worldwide?

A. Renal anaemia
B. Tumour anaemia
C. A and B Both
D. None of above

22.

Granulocyte colony stimulating factor stimulates proliferation and differentiation of neutrophil precursor cells to which form of cells?

A. Basophils
B. Reticulocytes
C. Immature neutrophils
D. Mature granulocytes

23.

Which branch of science is the study of the variations in a patient's response to drugs due to hereditary traits that may explain individual differences in the efficacy of drugs and in the occurrence of adverse drug reactions?

A. Pharmacogenetics

B. Pharmacocognacy
C. Medico-Legal Science
D. Haematology

24.

Any measurement that can predict a person's disease state or response to a drug treatment can be called a as what?

A. Enhancers
B. Enantiomers
C. Biomarker
D. Indicative

25.

The Bill and Melinda Gates Foundation sponsored the which forum and the forum also issued the report titled Improved Diagnostic Techniques for the Developing World?

A. Global Health Diagnostic
B. Global e learning
C. Public Health Organization
D. World Health Organization

26.

Stem cells are which type of that have the capacity to self-renew and to achieve multilineage differentiation?

A. Differentiated cells
B. Undifferentiated cells
C. Normal Cells
D. None of above

27.

Micro-arrays are miniaturised which type of supports?

A. Liquid supports
B. Semi Solid supports
C. Solid supports
D. None of above

28.

Arising from the previously described techniques, it was possible in 1995 to determine the first complete genome or DNA sequence of a free-living organism, the bacterium called by which name from following options?

A. *E.Coli*
B. *Pseudomonas*
C. *Haemophilus influenzae*
D. *Streptococcus*

29.

It has long been recognised that genes can be silenced by means of which technology?

A. Recombinant RNA
B. Recombinant DNA
C. Microarray
D. Antisense technology

30.

Transcription of antisense genes produces an RNA molecule that is complementary to the sense in which of following sequence?

A. DNA
B. RNA
C. cDNA
D. ssDNA

31.

Which technology was used in transgenic plants to control ripening–the FlavrSavr tomato?

A. Recombinant RNA
B. Recombinant DNA
C. Microarray
D. Antisense technology

32.

The anti-sense technology can do which effect on genes using double-stranded complementary synthetic oligonucleotides?

A. Silence
B. Activate
C. Mutated
D. None of above

33.

The discovery in 1993 of a gene expressing small non-protein coding RNAs in a small worm led to the discovery of a previously unknown class of endogenous, single-stranded 19–21 nucleotide molecules called micro RNAs (miRNAs) that can regulate up to 30% of mammalian genes, what is name of that worm?

A. *Coenorhabditis elegans*

B. Ascaries

C. Earthworm

D. None of above

34.

The discoverer, Craig Mells, was awarded in 2006 the Nobel Prize in which subject for his discovery of micro RNAs (miRNAs)?

A. Biology

B. Botany

C. Physiology and Medicine

D. Zoology and life science

35.

In biotechnological processes how many way/ways of growing microorganisms in the bioreactor?

A. Batch

B. Fed-batch

C. Continuous

D. All the above

36.

In a batch culture the microorganisms are inoculated into how much volume of medium and as growth takes place nutrients are consumed and products of growth (biomass, metabolites) accumulate?

A. Fixed Volume

B. Continuous increasing volume

C. Conthnuous decreasing volume

D. Both in increasing and decreasing volumes

37.

In case of batch growth of microorganisms the initial lag phase is a time of no apparent growth, but actual biochemical analyses what actually show in context of metabolic turnover?

A. Indicating that the cells are in the process of adapting to the environmental conditions
B. Indicating that the cells will divide slower
C. Indicating that the cells will not divide in new environmental conditions
D. None of above

38.

In case of protoplast fusion techniques which used with many microbial cells as well as with plant and animal cells, how we can increase the fusion rates

A. Assimilation Process
B. Extraction Processed
C. Polyethylene Dimer
D. Fusogen polyethylene glycol.

39.

What is short name of Brazil's National Ethanol Programme which was in response to the oil shock of the 1970s and has now succeeded in reducing the country's dependence on fossil fuel?

A. PROALCOOL
B. PROALCOAL
C. PROALCEEL
D. PROALCEOL

40.

Which car is the only one in the world that can use 100% of either bioethanol or gasoline?

A. Brazil's flex fuel car
B. Japans Honda N-Box mini car (kei)
C. Maruti Suzuki small cars
D. None of above

41.

The EU, particularly France, Italy and Germany, have been the leading proponents of biodiesel – France for agricultural reasons, Italy for environmental reasons and Germany which reasons?

A. Agricultural
B. Environmental
C. Both A and B
D. None of above

42.

The USA is the world's largest producer of biodiesel, mainly from which crop?

A. Sweet Corns
B. Rice
C. Wheat
D. Soybeans

43.

An exciting new industrial programme in the USA will combine bioethanol production with biodiesel production using which crop?

A. Sweet Corns
B. Rice
C. Wheat
D. Soybeans

44.

Domestic cattle are the major contributors producing methane gas about 75% of all animal emissions whereas humans produce about how much percentage?

A. 0.99
B. 0.25
C. 0.15
D. 0.4

45.

After carbon dioxide, which gas is considered to be the next most important greenhouse gas and is expected to contribute 18% of future warming?

A. Carbon monoxide
B. Methane
C. Ethane
D. Acetone

46.

Biogas is produced via which process and the process is a self-regulating symbiotic microbial process operating under anaerobic conditions, and functions best at temperatures around 30◦C?

A. Bio transition

B.   Bio assimilation
C.   Biodegradation
D.   Biomethanation

47.

Under ideal conditions, 10kg dry organic matter can produce $3m^3$ of biogas, which will provide 3h cooking, 3h lighting or how much hours of refrigeration with suitable equipment?

A.   3 hours
B.   10 hours
C.   24 hours
D.   5 days

48.

China is the largest user with over 7 million biogas units providing the equivalent energy of 22 million tons of coal, and with current subsidies a biogas plant in China is cheaper than which of following option?

A.   A car
B.   a bicycle
C.   a bike
D.   a truck

49.

Organic chemicals that cannot easily be degraded by microorganisms or are indeed totally resistant to attack are termed as what?

A.   Reasonable
B.   Rectify

C. Remainant

D. Recalcitrant

50.

Nowadays, plant scientists use thermal neutrons, X-rays or ethyl methane sulphate (a harsh carcinogenic chemical) that can damage DNA – to generate artificial mutations in crop plants, especially in which crop out of following?

A. Corn

B. Wheat

C. Cotton

D. Cereals

1. D	2. B	3. A	4. A	5. D	6. D	7. A	8. C	9. B	10. C
11. D	12. A	13. B	14. D	15. A	16. A	17. A	18. A	19. B	20. C
21. C	22. D	23. A	24. C	25. A	26. B	27. C	28. C	29. D	30. B
31. D	32. A	33. A	34. A	35. D	36. A	37. A	38. D	39. A	40. A
41. C	42. D	43. A	44. D	45. B	46. D	47. C	48. B	49. D	50. D

ANSWERS OF CHAPTER 7

CHAPTER VIII

Lipids and Cholesterol

1. Triacylglycerols are degraded by lipoprotein lipase, converting VLDL to which one of the following?

A. HDL
B. VLDL
C. LDL
D. Chylomicrons

2.

HDL removes cholesterol from the blood, carrying it to which organ?

A. Liver
B. Kidneys
C. Smooth Muscles
D. Skin

3.

Dietary conditions or genetic defects in cholesterol metabolism may lead to which disease?

A. Atherosclerosis
B. Heart disease
C. Both A and B
D. Rheumatic Fever

4.

Two products lovastatin and compactin, are used to treat patients with familial hypercholesterolemia derived from which of the following organism?

A. Fungi
B. Bacteria
C. Viruses
D. Fishes

5.

Lovastatin treatment lowers serum cholesterol by as much as how much in individuals having one defective copy of the gene for the LDL receptor?

A. 20%
B. 10%
C. 5%
D. 30%

6.

Lovastatin when combined with an edible resin that binds bile acids and prevents their reabsorption from the intestine, the drug than become what?

A. is even more effective
B. is less effective
C. moderately effective
D. non effective

7.

In familial HDL deficiency, HDL levels are very low; they are almost undetectable in which of the following disease?

A. Ischemic Disease
B. Diabetes
C. Hyper-cholestrolemia
D. Tangier disease

8.

Steroid hormones are effective at very low concentrations and are therefore synthesized in relatively small quantities. In comparison with the bile salts, their production consumes how much cholesterol?

A. Relatively little
B. Relatively higher
C. No cholesterol
D. Too High cholesterol

9.

Synthesis of steroid hormones requires removal of some or all of the carbons in the "side chain" on which carbon atom of the D ring of cholesterol?

A. C-20
B. C-17
C. C-22
D. C-29

10.

Chylomicrons, connection with the movement of dietary triacylglycerol from the intestine to which of the following options?

A. Other tissues
B. Bones

C. Bone marrow

D. Eyes

11.

Chylomicrons are the largest of the lipoproteins and the least dense, containing a high proportion of which of following?

A. HDL

B. VLDL

C. Triacylglycerol

D. LDL

12.

What is site for the Chylomicrons are synthesized?

A. ER of epithelial cells that line the small intestine

B. Inner lining cells of stomach

C. Inner wall of Oesophagus

D. None of above

13.

Chylomicrons after synthesis move through the lymphatic system and where it enter via the left subclavian vein?

A. Heart

B. Kidneys

C. Bloodstream

D. Bone Marrow

14.

The apolipoproteins of chylomicrons include apoE, and apoC-II and which one more from following?

A. apoB-40
B. apoB-38
C. apoB-58
D. apoB-48

15.

ApoC-II activates lipoprotein lipase in the capillaries of adipose, heart, skeletal muscle, and lactating mammary tissues, allowing the release of which compound from following to these tissues?

A. free fatty acids
B. free amino acids
C. free lipids
D. free minerals

16.

Different combinations of lipids and which one option out of following can produce particles of different densities, ranging from chylomicrons to high-density lipoproteins?

A. Fats
B. Proteins
C. Carbohydrates
D. Minerals

17.

Almost all fatty acids, the hydrocarbon components of many lipids, have an even number of carbon atoms (usually

12 to 24); they are either saturated or unsaturated, with double bonds almost always in the which configuration out of following?

A. Trans
B. Cis
C. Mixed
D. None

18.

Triacylglycerols contain how many fatty acid molecules esterified to the three hydroxyl groups of glycerol?

A. 2
B. 3
C. 4
D. 5

19.

Simple triacylglycerols contain how many type of fatty acid in comparison to mixed triacylglycerols which may contain two or three types?

A. Only one
B. Zero
C. Only two
D. Only Three

20.

Triacylglycerols are primarily which type of fats, present in many foods?

A. VLDL

B. Cholesterol

C. Free fatty acids

D. Storage fats

21.

The central architectural feature of biological membranes is a how many layered lipids, which acts as a barrier to the passage of polar molecules and ions?

A. Triple

B. Double

C. Single

D. None

22.

Membrane lipids are amphipathic: one end of the molecule is hydrophobic, the other of which type?

A. Hydrophilic

B. Hydrophobic

C. Both A and B

D. None

23.

In case of glycerophospholipids the hydrophobic regions are composed of how many fatty acids joined to glycerol?

A. One

B. Two

C. Three

D. Four

24.

Some animal tissues and some unicellular organisms are rich in ether lipids, in which one of the two acyl chains is attached to glycerol in ether, rather than which common linkage?

A. Ester
B. Alcohol
C. Phenol
D. None

25.

In the alkyl ether lipids,the ether-linked chain may be saturated and in plasmalogens it may contain a double bond between which carbon atoms?

A. C-1 and C-2
B. C-3 and C-4
C. C-5 and C-6
D. C-7 and C-8

26.

Vertebrate heart tissue is uniquely enriched in ether lipids; about half of the heart phospholipids are of which type out of following?

A. Sphingolipids
B. Steroids
C. Plasmalogens
D. Chylomicrons

27.

Which option out of following resembles phosphatidylcholines in their general properties and three-dimensional structure?

A. Sphingomyelins
B. Steroids
C. Plasmalogens
D. Chylomicrons

28.

Cerebrosides have a single sugar linked to which option out of following; those with galactose are characteristically found in the plasma membranes of cells in neural tissue, and those with glucose in the plasma membranes of cells in nonneural tissues?

A. Cephalin
B. Ceramide
C. Both A and B
D. None

29.

What is the nature of Globosides, which are glycosphingolipids with two or more sugars, usually D-glucose, D-galactose, or N-acetyl-D-galactosamine?

A. Positive charged
B. Negative charged
C. Neutral (uncharged)
D. None of above

30.

Cerebrosides and globosides are sometimes called neutral glycolipids, as they have no charge at which pH out of following?

A. pH 9
B. pH 5
C. pH 4
D. pH 7

31.

Sialic acid gives gangliosides the negative charge at which pH from following options, that distinguishes them from globosides?

A. pH 9
B. pH 5
C. pH 4
D. pH 7

32.

When sphingolipids were discovered a century ago by which physician-chemist?

A. Johann Thudichum
B. Johnson
C. H Khorana
D. J Dalton

33.

In humans, how many different sphingolipids have been identified in cellular membranes?

A. 40
B. 45
C. 55
D. 60

34.

The carbohydrate moieties of certain sphingolipids define which of the following in human blood?

A. Blood groups
B. Antigens
C. Antibodies
D. None of above

35.

Bile acids are polar derivatives of cholesterol that act as detergents in the intestine, emulsifying dietary fats to make them more readily accessible for which enzyme?

A. Lipases
B. Proteases
C. Trypsin
D. None

36.

The phosphatidylethanolamine and phosphatidylcholines belongs to which type?

A. Glycerophospholipids
B. Phosphates
C. Sterols
D. Pure Fats

37.

The polar heads of the glycerophospholipids carry electric charges at which pH?

A. near pH 7
B. near pH 9

C. near pH 10

D. near pH 3

38.

Which option out of following has unique membrane lipids, with long-chain alkyl groups ether-linked to glycerol at both ends and with sugar residues and/or phosphate joined to the glycerol to provide a polar or charged head group?

A. Yeast

B. *Staphylococcus aureus*

C. *E.coli*

D. *Archaebacteria*

39.

Steroid hormones move through the bloodstream from their site of production to target tissues, they require which type of carrier?

A. carbohydrate carriers

B. Mineral carriers

C. enzymes carriers

D. protein carriers

40.

Prednisone and prednisolone are steroid drugs with which type of activities, mediated in part by the inhibition of arachidonate release by phospholipase A_2?

A. Anti-viral

B. Anti-bacterial

C. potent anti-inflammatory

D. potent anti-fungal

41.

There are three classes of eicosanoids: prostaglandins, thromboxanes, and which one more from following options?

A. Lectins
B. Lencithil
C. Lymphatics
D. Leukotrienes

42.

Prostaglandins (PG) contain a how many carbon ring originating from the chain of arachidonic acid?

A. Six
B. Five
C. Four
D. Three

43.

Two groups of prostaglandins were originally defined: PGE, for ether-soluble, and PGF soluble in which buffer?

A. Bicine
B. Acetate Buffer
C. Phosphate buffer
D. None of Above

44.

The thromboxaneshave a six-membered ring containing ether are product of which cells?

A. Platelets
B. Neutrophils
C. Lymphocytes
D. Eosinophil

45.

The nonsteroidal antiinflammatory drugs (NSAIDs)—aspirin, ibuprofen, and meclofenamate, were shown by John Vane to inhibit the which enzyme?

A. Lipases
B. Proteases
C. Hexokinase
D. Prostaglandin H2 synthase

46.

Leukotrienes, first found in leukocytes, contain how many conjugated double bonds?

A. Two
B. Three
C. Four
D. One

47.

The strong contraction of the smooth muscles of the lung that occurs during anaphylactic shock is part of the potentially fatal allergic reaction in individuals hypersensitive to which of the following?

A. Bee stings
B. Penicillin
C. Both A and B

D. None of Above

48.

Vascular plants contain phosphatidylinositol 4,5-bisphosphate, as well as the phospholipase that releases IP_3, and they use IP_3 to regulate the intracellular concentration of which of following ion?

A. Mg++
B. Ca^{2+}
C. Na^+
D. K^+

49.

Brassinolide and the related group of brassino steroids are functionally of which type in plants?

A. Potent growth regulators
B. Stem Water dryer
C. Water remover
D. Root enhancer

50.

Which ester of jasmonate gives the characteristic fragrance of jasmine oil, which is widely used in the perfume industry?

A. Methyl
B. Ethyl
C. Acetate
D. Propyl

1. C	2. A	3. C	4. A	5. D	6. A	7. D	8. A	9. B	10. A
11. C	12. A	13. C	14. D	15. A	16. B	17. B	18. B	19. A	20. D
21. B	22. A	23. B	24. A	25. A	26. C	27.	28. B	29. C	30. D
31. D	32. A	33. D	34. A	35. A	36. A	37. A	38. D	39. D	40. C
41. D	42. B	43. C	44. A	45. D	46. B	47. C	48. B	49. A	50. A

ANSWERS OF CHAPTER 8

CHAPTER IX

Proteins and Proteomics

1. Rieske iron-sulfur proteins (named after their discoverer, John S. Rieske), in this protein one Fe atom is coordinated to which residues rather than two Cys residues?

A. Two His
B. Three Lys
C. Two Glu
D. Two Leu

2.
In the overall reaction catalyzed by the mitochondrial respiratory chain, electrons move from NADH, succinate, or some other primary electron donor through flavoproteins, ubiquinone, iron-sulfur proteins, and cytochromes, and finally to which out of following?

A. CO_2
B. O_2
C. H_2
D. CO
3.

Protein structure is stabilized by what type of interactions?

A. multiple strong interactions
B. multiple weak interactions

C. multiple covalent interactions

D. None

4.

Which type of interactions are the major contributors to stabilizing the globular form of most soluble proteins?

A. Hydrophilic

B. Hydrophobic

C. Ionic

D. Covalent

5.

The term "tertiary structure" of proteins refers to the entire three dimensional conformation of which of following?

A. R-group

B. a amino acid

C. a polypeptide

D. none of above

6.

The α-keratins have evolved for what?

A. Strength

B. Weakness

C. Delicacy

D. None

7.

Which Proteins constitute almost the entire dry weight of hair, wool, nails, claws, quills, horns, hooves, and much of the outer layer of skin?

A. α-keratins
B. α-Ketoacids
C. Phospholipids
D. Glyceroprotins

8.

Name the process is a common mechanism by which proteins are anchored to the inner surface of cellular membranes in mammals.

A. Prenylation
B. Aeration
C. Atomization
D. None

9.

Cholesterol is formed from which of the following in a complex series of reactions?

A. Sphingolipids
B. Acetyl-CoA
C. NADPH
D. ATP

10.

The Stokes radius is a function of molecular which of following parameters?

A. mass and shape
B. size and weight
C. volume and weight
D. None

11.

Growth Hormone promotes which type of growth by stimulating hepatic production of proteins?

A. Skeletal growth
B. Muscle growth
C. Skin growth
D. None

12.

Thyroid-deficient infants may suffer irreversible brain damage may cause cretinism while thyroid deficiency in adults is termed as what?

A. Malnutrition
B. Myxedema
C. Wrinkled skin
D. Anaemia

13.

Non-ruminant animals, including humans, obtain proteins principally from whom and their products out of following?

A. Animals
B. Plants
C. Micro-organisms
D. Yeast

14.

Which is the simplest amino acid in which R is a hydrogen atom?

A. Alanine
B. Glycine
C. Ornithine
D. Tyrosine

15.

Organelles move through the cytoplasm along which of the following options and their motion powered by energy dependent motor proteins?

A. Protein filaments
B. Cartilages
C. Hairs
D. None

16.

Cytoskeletal proteins assemble into which filaments that give cells shape and rigidity and serve as rails along which cellular organelles move throughout the cell?

A. Long
B. Short
C. Medium
D. None

17.

Proteins and nucleic acids are which type of macromolecules?

A. Structural macromolecules
B. Informational macromolecules
C. Uniform macromolecules
D. None

18.

Louis Pasteur encountered the phenomenon of which type of activity in 1843, during his investigation of the crystalline sediment that accumulated in wine casks?

A. Atomic activity
B. Optical activity
C. Photometric activity
D. None

19.

What is name of the ability to distinguish between stereoisomers which is a property of enzymes and other proteins and a characteristic feature of the molecular logic of living cells?

A. Stereo specificity
B. Optical Activity
C. Atomic Activity
D. None

20.

Proteins are not stored for later use, so excess proteins must be converted into which of the following options and used to supply energy or build energy reserves?

A. Glucose
B. Triglycerides

C. Both A and B

D. None

21.

When protein-rich foods enter the stomach, they are greeted by a mixture of the enzyme pepsin and hydrochloric acid, what is the percentage of acid?

A. 0.5 per cent

B. 1 per cent

C. 1.5 per cent

D. 2 per cent

22.

When the food-gastric juice mixture (chyme) enters the small intestine, the pancreas releases which chemical to neutralize the HCl?

A. Sodium bicarbonate

B. Hydrochloric acid

C. Acetone

D. Albumin

23.

In the pancreas, which of the following store trypsin and chymotrypsin as trypsinogen and chymotrypsinogen?

A. Intra-cellular

B. Vesicles

C. Golgi Bodies

D. None

24.

Once released into the small intestine, an enzyme found in the wall of the small intestine, called as what, which can binds to trypsinogen and converts it into its active form, trypsin?

A. Lipase
B. Enterokinase
C. Glucose Oxidase
D. None

25.

Urea Cycle occurs primarily in which organ and also to a lesser extent, in the kidney?

A. Bones
B. Liver
C. Gall Bladder
D. None

26.

Amino acids can also be used as a source of energy, especially in times of which conditions?

A. Starvation
B. Exercise
C. Excessive Eating
D. None

27.

Pyruvate dehydrogenase complex deficiency (PDCD) and phenylketonuria (PKU) are which type of disorders?

A. Genetic disorders

B. Metabolic Disorder

C. Infectious Disorder

D. None

28.

PKU affects about 1 in how many births in the United States?

A. 15,000

B. 20,000

C. 25,000

D. 30,000

29.

People afflicted with Phenylketonuria lack sufficient activity of the enzyme phenylalanine hydroxylase and are therefore unable to break down phenylalanine into which amino acids adequately?

A. Tyrosine

B. Threonine

C. Alanine

D. Glycine

30.

Digestion of proteins begins in the __________ where __________ and __________ mix with food to break down protein into __________.

A. stomach; amylase; HCl; amino acids

B. mouth; pepsin; HCl; fatty acids

C. stomach; lipase; HCl; amino acids

D. stomach; pepsin; HCl; amino acids

31.

Chymotrypsin is which type of enzyme that digests protein?

A. Hepatic enzymes
B. Pancreatic enzyme
C. Kidney enzymes
D. Intestinal enzymes

32.

What is the type of Chymotrypsinogen that is activated by trypsin into chymotrypsin?

A. Isoenzyme
B. Alloenzyme
C. Proenzyme
D. Co-factor

33.

What is the amount of proteins present in Plant cells in comparison with animal cells?

A. High
B. Equivalent
C. Low
D. Non Predictable

34.

Shorter polymers of sugars (oligosaccharides) attached to proteins or lipids at the cell surface serve for which of the following work?

A. Cell Wall Strength

B. Specific cellular signals

C. Cell Replication

D. None

35.

The amino acids in proteins occur only as their which type of isomers and glucose occurs only as its D isomer?

A. L

B. D

C. Changing between L and D

D. Both A and B same time

36.

During rapid cell growth the precursors of proteins and nucleic acids must be made in which quantities?

A. Small quantities

B. Large quantities

C. Moderate quantities

D. None

37.

The precise three dimensional structures or native conformation, of the protein is to its function?

A. Non-Important

B. Most Important

C. Less Important

D. None

38.

When two genes share readily detectable sequence similarities (nucleotide sequence in DNA or amino acid sequence in the proteins they encode), their sequences are said to be what?

A. Homologous
B. Orthologous
C. Isomers
D. Stereomers

39.

If two homologous genes occur in the same species, what they are said to be?

A. Paralogous
B. Analogous
C. Orthologous
D. None

40.

Paralogous genes are presumed to have been derived by gene duplication followed by gradual changes in the sequences how many copies?

A. Single
B. Both
C. Recessive gene copy only
D. Dominant gene copy only

41.

Typically, paralogous proteins are similar not only in sequence but also which of the following options?

A. Sequences
B. Amino acids
C. 3-D structure
D. None

42.

Two homologous genes (or proteins) found in different species are said to be what?

A. Paralogous
B. Analogous
C. Orthologous
D. None

43.

The genome of an insect should contain genes that encode proteins involved in specifying the characteristic insect segmented body plan but these genes not present in which of the following?

A. Cockroach
B. Yeast
C. Grass Hopper
D. None

44.

The components for the first cell were produced by the action of lightning and high temperature on simple atmospheric molecules such as CO_2 and which compound?

A. NH_3
B. NH_2
C. CO

D. H_2O

45.

Many biomolecules are amphipathic; proteins, pigments, certain vitamins, and the sterols and phospholipids of membranes all have which type of surface regions?

A. Polar
B. Non-Polar
C. Both A and B
D. None

46.

Hydrophobic interactions among lipids, and between lipids and proteins, are the most important determinants of structure in which of the following?

A. Cellular components
B. Mitochondria
C. Biological membranes
D. None

47.

The binding of a hormone or a neurotransmitter to its cellular receptor protein is the result of which type of interactions?

A. Strong
B. Weak
C. Medium Strength
D. None of above

48.

For many proteins, tightly bound water molecules are essential to their function. In a reaction central to the process of photosynthesis, for example, light drives protons across a biological membrane as electrons flow through a series of electron-carrying proteins, one of these proteins, cytochrome f, has a chain of how many bound water molecules?

A. Six
B. Seven
C. Five
D. Nine

49.

The high concentration of albumin and other proteins in blood plasma contributes to its which property?

A. Osmolarity
B. Osmosis
C. Ionic Strength
D. None of above

50.

Ionic interactions are among the forces that do what to a protein molecule and allow an enzyme to recognize and bind its substrate?

A. Disrupts
B. Stabilize
C. Reorganize
D. None of above

1. A	2. B	3. A	4. B	5. C	6. A	7. A	8. A	9. B	10. A
11. A	12. B	13. A	14. B	15. A	16. A	17. B	18. B	19. A	20. C
21. A	22. A	23. B	24. B	25. B	26. A	27. A	28. A	29. A	30. D
31. B	32. C	33. C	34. B	35. A	36. B	37. B	38. A	39. A	40. B
41. C	42. C	43. B	44. A	45. C	46. C	47. B	48. C	49. A	50. B

ANSWERS OF CHAPTER 9

CHAPTER X

Enzymology

1.

In vitro studies of pure enzymes commonly performed at which concentration of enzymes out of following options?

A. High
B. Low
C. Moderate
D. None

2.

Virtually every chemical reaction in a cell occurs at a significant rate only because of the presence of which of the following?

A. Growth Factor
B. Vitamins
C. Enzymes
D. Acids

3.

Enzymes typically show maximal catalytic activity at a characteristic pH, called the what?

A. Lowered pH
B. Higher pH
C. pH optimum

D. Normal Ph

4.

Myoglobin is a single polypeptide of how many amino acid residues with one molecule of heme?

A. 143
B. 153
C. 133
D. 123

5.

Acetyl-CoA carboxylase in the bacteria has how many separate polypeptide subunits?

A. Two
B. Three
C. Four
D. Five

6.

In hepatocytes and adipocytes, cytosolic NADPH is largely generated by the pentose phosphate pathway and by which enzyme?

A. G6PD
B. GOD
C. POD
D. Malic enzyme

7.

When animals ingest an excess of certain polyunsaturated fatty acids, the expression of genes encoding a wide range of lipogenic enzymes in the liver is affected, choose a right option for this effect?

A. Increased
B. Activated
C. Suppressed
D. Denatured

8.

Aspirin inhibits which of the following as it is also used in low doses to treat patients at risk of heart attacks?

A. Lipid lowering
B. Platelet aggregation and blood clotting
C. Blood formation
D. Suppression of WBC activities

9.

COX-1 and COX-2 are mammals which type of enzymes?

A. Cofactors
B. Iso-enzymes
C. Metalloproteinase
D. Oxidases

10.

COX-1 is responsible for the synthesis of the prostaglandins that regulate the secretion of gastric mucin, and COX2 for the prostaglandins that mediate which of following?

A. Inflammation

B. Pain
C. Fever
D. All the above
11.

Aspirin inhibits which of the following?

A. COX 1
B. COX 2
C. Both A and B
D. None
12.

Ubiquinone (also called coenzyme Q, or simply Q) benzoquinone with a long isoprenoid side chain is soluble in which of following?

A. Water
B. Lipid
C. Both A and B
D. None
13.

The cytochromes are proteins with characteristic strong absorption of which type of light due to their iron containing heme prosthetic groups?

A. Ultraviolet
B. Visible
C. Infra-Red
D. None
14.

The closely related compounds plastoquinone (of plant chloroplasts) and menaquinone (of bacteria) play roles which type to that of ubiquinone?

A. Analogous
B. Opposite
C. Non-related
D. None

15.

In iron-sulfur proteins, first discovered by Helmut Beinert, the iron is present not in heme but in association with which of the following option/s?

A. inorganic sulfur atoms
B. sulfur atoms of Cys residues in the protein
C. Both A and B
D. None

16.

Obligate anaerobes are the organisms that they die when exposed to which gas?

A. Oxygen
B. Nitrogen
C. Hydrogen
D. Carbon-Di-Oxide

17.

In general sense most enzymes are of which type of proteins?

A. Globular

B. Threaded
C. Plates
D. None

18.

Which are the terms also used to refer to the low affinity and high-affinity conformations of allosteric enzymes, respectively?

A. Q and P
B. W and D
C. T and R
D. X and Z

19.

Myoglobin can be detected in plasma following a myocardial infarction, but assay of which of the following provides a more sensitive index of myocardial injury?

A. Serum Minerals
B. Serum Enzymes
C. Serum Urea
D. Serum Albumin

20.

With the exception of a few catalytic RNA molecules, or ribozymes, the vast majority of enzymes belong to which of the following?

A. Carbohydrates
B. Proteins
C. Vitamins
D. Minerals

21.

In general, an enzyme's name consists of a term that identifies the type of reaction catalyzed followed by which word as suffix?

A. –ase
B. –ace
C. –axe
D. –and

22.

The International Union of Biochemists (IUB) developed a complex but unambiguous system of enzyme nomenclature. In the IUB system, each enzyme has a unique name and code number that reflect what?

A. The type of reaction catalysed and the substrates involved
B. The intensity of reaction catalysed and the product involved
C. The heat of reaction catalysed and the product involved
D. The intensity of reaction catalysed and the substrate involved

23.

In many enzymes which out of following are the most common prosthetic groups?

A. Metals
B. Gas
C. –OH
D. –CO

24.

What is the nature of an enzyme?

A. Vitamin
B. Lipid
C. Carbohydrate
D. Protein

25.

What is an apoenzyme?

A. It is a protein portion of an enzyme
B. It is a non-protein group
C. It is a complete, biologically active conjugated enzyme
D. It is a prosthetic group

26.

Name the enzyme secreted by pancreas?

A. Pepsin
B. Chymotrypsin
C. Trypsin
D. Alcohol dehydrogenase

27.

Mark the CORRECT function of enzyme, Peptidase?

A. Cleave phosphodiester bond
B. Cleave amino bonds
C. Remove phosphate from a substrate
D. Removal of H_2O

28.

Which of the following function is catalyzed by Racemases?

A. Removal of water
B. Intramolecular transfer of a functional group
C. Interconversion of L and D stereoisomers
D. Inversion of asymmetric carbon atom

29.

Which of the following is an example of ligases enzyme?

A. Mutases
B. Epimerases
C. Racemases
D. Carboxylases

30.

What is the binding energy?

A. Free energy released in the formation of enzyme-substrate interaction
B. The energy required to form a bond
C. The energy required to bind substrate
D. It is the activation energy

31.

Which of the following is INCORRECT for the lock-and-key model?

A. It is used to describe the binding process
B. The active site of the enzyme is complementary to the substrate
C. It demonstrates enzyme-substrate complex

D. The binding of the substrate produces a conformational change in enzyme

32.

Which of the following is not a catalytic strategy for an enzyme to perform specific reaction?

A. Covalent catalysis
B. Metal ion catalysis
C. Michaelis constant
D. Acid-base catalysis

33.

Which of the following is not an example of irreversible enzyme inhibitor?

A. Cyanide
B. Sarin
C. Diisopropyl phosphoflouridate (DIPF)
D. Statin drugs

34.

Lineweaver-Burk plot is also known as________

A. Double reciprocal plot
B. Hanes-Woolf plot
C. Eadie-Hofstee plot
D. Steady-state equation

35.

What is an Isozyme?

A. Same structure, different function

B. Different structure, the same function
C. Same structure, the same function
D. Different structure, different function

36.

This cytochrome is usually present where in the cell?

A. Smooth ER
B. Mitochondria
C. Golgi Bodies
D. Cytoplasm

37.

Eicosanoids are belongs to which type of molecules from following options?

A. Potent biological signalling
B. Potent Toxicants
C. Inhibitors
D. Mutants

38.

Which renal enzyme, is secreted when the renal oxygen level falls?

A. Erythropoietic factor
B. Lipase
C. Amylase
D. Urease

39.

Renal Erythropoietic factor enzyme reacts with a plasma protein to form erythropoietin, which subsequently stimulates the bone marrow to produce more which cells?

A. WBCs
B. RBCs
C. Platelets
D. Immunoglobulins

40.

Give name an enzyme contained in RBCs?

A. Carbonic anhydrase
B. Amylase
C. Lipase
D. Isomerase

41.

Glucose-6-phosphate dehydrogenase is an enzyme pivotal in generating which of the following through the pentose pathway in glucose metabolism?

A. ATP
B. NADPH
C. ADP
D. MNP

42.

In comparison to older RBCs the Younger one has which concentration of enzymes?

A. Lower
B. Higher
C. Equal
D. Absent

43.

Leukocyte alkaline phosphatase, an enzyme found in which cell out of following?

A. Neutrophils
B. Monocytes
C. Platelets
D. RBCs

44.

The periodic acid–Schiff stain, which tests for enzymes found in granulocytes and which one more cell?

A. Stem cells
B. Platelets
C. Erythrocytes
D. Hepatic Cells

45.

In the fibrinolytic system, fibrin strands are broken down into progressively smaller fragments by a proteolytic enzyme named as what?

A. Plasmin
B. Kinase
C. Actin
D. Trypsin

46.

Which Enzyme estimation is indicative of Breast, pulmonary carcinoma?

A. Creatine kinase isoenzyme (CK-BB)

B. Lactate Dehydrogenase (LDH)
C. Alaklaine Phosphatase (ALP)
D. Glucose Oxidase (GOD)

47.

Which Enzyme estimation is indicative of Pancreatic carcinoma?

A. Galactosyltransferase (GT II)
B. Creatine kinase isoenzyme (CK-BB)
C. Lactate Dehydrogenase (LDH)
D. Alaklaine Phosphatase (ALP)

48.

Aspartate aminotransferase (AST), formerly known as glutamic-oxaloacetic transaminase (GOT), catalyzes the reversible transfer of which group between the amino acid, aspartate, and α-ketoglutamic acid?

A. Keto Group
B. Amino Group
C. Carboxylic Group
D. Ether Group

49.

In which disease infusion of albumin of placental origin took place?

A. Paget's disease
B. Haemolytic Disease of new born
C. Sickle Cell Anaemia
D. Thalassemia

50.

Leucine aminopeptidase (LAP), an isoenzyme of which of the following enzyme?

A. Alkaline phosphatase
B. Galactosyltransferase
C. Creatine kinase isoenzyme
D. Lactate Dehydrogenase

1. B	2. C	3. C	4. B	5. B	6. D	7. C	8. B	9. B	10. D
11. C	12. B	13. B	14. B	15. C	16. A	17. A	18. C	19. B	20. B
21. A	22. A	23. A	24. D	25. A	26. C	27. B	28. C	29. D	30. A
31. D	32. C	33. D	34. A	35. B	36. A	37. A	38. A	39. B	40. A
41. B	42. B	43. A	44. C	45. A	46. A	47. A	48. B	49. A	50. A

ANSWERS OF CHAPTER 10

CHAPTER XI

Metabolism

1.

Who developed chemical methods to synthesize polyribonucleotides with defined, repeating sequences of two to four bases?

A. H. Gobind Khorana
B. J C Bose
C. James Watson
D. Thomson

2.

Thioalcohols (thiols), in which the oxygen atom of an alcohol is replaced with which atom?

A. a carbon atom
B. a sulfur atom
C. a phosphorous atom
D. a hydrogen atom

3.

The tendency to achieve the highest degree of randomness, expressed as what?

A. Enthalpy
B. Entropy
C. Epitope
D. Empty

4.

Phosphoenolpyruvate contains a phosphate ester bond that undergoes hydrolysis to yield which enol form of following?

A. Pyruvate
B. Butarate
C. Phosphate
D. Acetate

5.

In aqueous solution ATP is thermodynamically in which state out of following?

A. Unstable
B. Stable
C. Non-Reactive
D. Carries more negative charges

6.

In the firefly, which is used out of following, in a set of reactions that converts chemical energy into light energy?

A. ADP
B. ADPH
C. ATP
D. NATP

7.

In the fire flies generation of a light flash requires activation of which of the following?

A. Actin
B. Lactin

C. Luciferin
D. Cytosol
8.

How much of the total energy consumed at rest is used to pump Na^+ and K^+ across plasma membranes via the Na^+-K^+ ATPase?

A. Three-fourth
B. Half
C. Two-third
D. One-fifth
9.

Which is the energy currency of the living cell?

A. ADP
B. ADPH
C. ATP
D. NATP
10.

In phosphocreatine, which bond can be hydrolysed to generate free creatine and Pi?

A. P-P
B. P-N
C. P-O
D. P-H
11.

When the blood glucose concentration is high, as it is after a meal rich in carbohydrates, excess glucose is transported into hepatocytes, where hexokinase IV converts it to which compound?

A. glucose 6-phosphate
B. Mannose
C. Fructose 6-phosphate
D. galactose

12.

Hexokinase IV (glucokinase) is sequestered in the nucleus of which cell?

A. Hepatocyte
B. Leucocytes
C. Reticulocytes
D. Nephrons

13.

Hexokinase IV (glucokinase) is released from nucleus when the cytosolic glucose concentration changes to which of following?

A. Rises
B. Decreases
C. Remain same
D. None

14.

Phosphofructokinase-1(PFK-1) is inhibited by which of the following?

A. ATP and citrate
B. ADP and nitrate

C. ADPH and pyruvate

D. NADP and Citrate

15.

Phosphofructokinase-1(PFK-1) is allosterically activated by which of the following?

A. fructose 2,6-bisphosphate

B. Fructose monophosphate

C. Mannose

D. Galactose

16.

Gluconeogenesis and glycolysis are not identical pathways running in which directions out of following?

A. Same

B. Opposite

C. Both directions

D. None

17.

How many enzymatic reactions out of the ten enzymatic reactions of gluconeogenesis are reverses of glycolytic reactions?

A. 9

B. 8

C. 7

D. 6

18.

Formation of one molecule of glucose from pyruvate requires 4 ATP, 2 GTP, and how many NADH?

A. 3
B. 4
C. 2
D. 5

19.

In mammals, gluconeogenesis in the liver and kidney provides glucose for use by the brain, muscles, and which out of following?

A. Bones
B. Cartilages
C. Erythrocytes
D. Cornea

20.

Animals cannot convert acetyl-CoA derived from which out of following into glucose?

A. Fatty acids
B. Amino Acids
C. Urea
D. Creatinine

21.

Which is the first reaction of the pentose phosphate pathway out of following?

A. Oxidation of glucose 6-phosphate
B. Reduction of glucose 6-phosphate

C. Hydrogenation of glucose 6-phosphate

D. Acidification glucose 6-phosphate

22.

In favism disease, which occur out of following?

A. Breakdown of erythrocytes

B. Breaking of Muscles

C. Neuron degeneration

D. Toxication

23.

Most G6PDdeficient individuals are which type out of following?

A. Symptomatic

B. Asymptomatic

C. Severe ill

D. Aggressive

24.

G6PD catalyzes the first step in the pentose phosphate pathway and produces which out of following?

A. NADPH

B. ADH

C. ATP

D. AMP

25.

G6PD deficiency frequencies as high as 25% occur in tropical Africa, parts of the Middle East, and Southeast Asia, what is common in these areas out of following?

A. where malaria is most prevalent
B. where polio is most prevalent
C. where tuberculosis is most prevalent
D. where AIDS is most prevalent

26.

In vitro studies show that growth of which parasite is inhibited in G6PD-deficient erythrocytes?

A. *Plasmodium falciparum*
B. *Human immunodeficiency virus*
C. *Plasmodium vivax*
D. *Ascaries*

27.

The oxidative pentose phosphate pathway (phosphogluconate pathway or hexose monophosphate pathway) brings about oxidation and decarboxylation at which carbon atom of glucose 6-phosphate?

A. C-1
B. C-2
C. C-3
D. C-4

28.

Rapidly growing tissues and tissues carrying out active biosynthesis of fatty acids, cholesterol, or steroid hormones send which quantity of glucose 6-phosphate through the pentose phosphate pathway?

A. Less
B. Moderate

C. More

D. None

29.

Wernicke Korsakoff syndrome is which type of defect?

A. Genetic

B. Metabolic

C. Infectious

D. Contagious

30.

Arsenate is structurally and chemically similar to which of the following?

A. Sulphur

B. inorganic phosphate (Pi)

C. inorganic nitrate

D. Oxygen

31.

What is type of Phloridzin, obtained from the bark of the pear tree?

A. a toxic glycoside

B. a toxic protein

C. a toxic steroids

D. a toxic venom

32.

Lactate absorbed by the liver is converted to glucose, with the input of how much of ATP for every mole of glucose produced?

A. 6 mol
B. 8 mol
C. 10 mol
D. 12 mol

33.

Most of the biosynthetic activities in plants (including CO_2 assimilation) occur in which part of plants cells?

A. Plastids
B. Cell wall
C. Cell membrane
D. Nucleus

34.

Amyloplasts are one of the type of which of the following?

A. Green Plastids
B. Black Plastids
C. Colourless plastids
D. None

35.

Chloroplasts can be converted to which of the following by the loss of their internal membranes and chlorophyll?

A. Amyloplastid
B. Proplastids
C. Golgi Bodies
D. Mitochondria

36.

Which cycle is active in the germinating seeds of some plants and in certain microorganisms that can live on acetate as the sole carbon source?

A. Urea
B. Creatinine
C. Glyoxylate
D. None

37.

Glyoxylate cycle involves several citric acid cycle enzymes and two additional enzymes: isocitrate lyase and which one more from options below?

A. Hexokinase
B. Lipase
C. Hydrolase
D. Malate synthase

38.

Vertebrates lack the glyoxylate cycle and cannot synthesize glucose from which of the following?

A. Acetate
B. Malate
C. Proteins
D. Fatty Acids

39.

Beriberi, a disease caused by which vitamin deficiency?

A. Riboflavin
B. Thiamine

C. Vitamin C

D. Vitamin D

40.

Glutamate and glutamine play especially critical roles in nitrogen metabolism, acting as a kind of general collection point for which groups?

A. Acyl groups

B. Amino groups

C. Keto groups

D. Sulpha groups

41.

In humans, the degradation of ingested proteins to their constituent amino acids occurs in which of the following?

A. Liver

B. Oesophagus

C. Mouth

D. Gastrointestinal tract

42.

As the acidic stomach contents pass into the small intestine, the low pH triggers secretion of which hormone?

A. Pepsin

B. Secretin

C. Gastric Juice

D. Gastrin

43.

Hormone cholecystokinin, stimulates secretion of several which enzymes?

A. Intestinal
B. Hepatic
C. Pancreatic
D. Duodenal

44.

L-glutamate dehydrogenase in mammals, this enzyme is present in which of the following?

A. mitochondrial matrix
B. cell wall
C. cytoplasm
D. Golgi bodies

45.

Which is the first heart enzyme to appear in the blood after a heart attack?

A. Alanine Aminotransferase
B. Aspartate aminotransferase
C. Creatine kinase
D. Glucose Oxidase

46.

Proteases degrade ingested proteins in which of following?

A. Mouth
B. Stomach
C. Small intestine

D. Both B and C

47.

The pyruvate produced by deamination of alanine in the liver is converted to glucose, which is transported back to which organ as part of the glucose-alanine cycle?

A. Liver
B. Kidneys
C. Muscle
D. Heart

48.

The flux of nitrogen through the urea cycle in an individual animal varies with which of the following?

A. Diet
B. Exercise
C. Water Intake
D. None

49.

People with genetic defects in any enzyme involved in urea formation cannot tolerate which type of diets?

A. Fats rich
B. protein rich
C. carbohydrates rich
D. Vitamin rich

50.

The urea cycle results in a net conversion of oxaloacetate to fumarate, both of which are intermediates in which cycle?

A. Glycolysis
B. Citric acid
C. Glyogenolysis
D. Metabolic Mill

1. A	2. B	3. B	4. A	5. A	6. C	7. C	8. C	9. C	10. B
11. A	12. A	13. A	14. A	15. A	16. B	17. C	18. C	19. C	20. A
21. A	22. A	23. B	24. A	25. A	26. A	27. A	28. C	29. A	30. B
31. A	32. A	33. A	34. C	35. B	36. C	37. D	38. A	39. B	40. B
41. D	42. B	43. C	44. A	45. C	46. C	47. C	48. A	49. B	50. B

ANSWERS OF CHAPTER 11

CHAPTER XII

Molecular Biology

1.

The DNA that is the entire genetic material of *E. coli* is a single molecule, which contain how many nucleotide pairs?

A. 4.64 million
B. 3.64 million
C. 2.64 million
D. 1.64 million

2.

The classic experiment on the abiotic (non-biological) origin of organic biomolecules was carried out in 1953 by which scientist out of following?

A. Stanley Miller
B. J Thomson
C. H Khurana
D. Carolus Linnaeus

3.

Drosophila melanogaster is also famous as which name out of following?

A. Flower fly
B. Pet Fly
C. Fruit fly
D. Leaf Fly

4.

Two homologous genes (or proteins) found in different species are said to be what?

A. Homologous
B. Orthologous
C. Analogous
D. Chemologous

5.

The genomes of chimpanzees and humans are how much identical?

A. 70.9%
B. 80.9%
C. 99.9%
D. 50.9%

6.

In 1996, scientists working in Greenland found not fossil remains but chemical evidence of life from as far back as how many years old?

A. 3.85 billion
B. 2.85 billion
C. 1.85 billion
D. 0.85 billion

7.

The components for the first cell were produced by the action of lightning and high temperature on simple atmospheric molecules such as which of following?

A. CO_2 and NH_3
B. CO and NH_2
C. O_2 and H
D. Cl_2 and NH_2
8.

Bacterial cells have which rate of metabolism as compared to the animal cells?

A. Higher
B. Lower
C. Medium
D. Same
9.

Axonal processes can be as long as how much length?

A. 2 m
B. 1 m
C. 3 m
D. 1.5 m
10.

Pure L-ascorbic acid (vitamin C) extracted from rose hips is quality wise how much than pure L-ascorbic acid manufactured in a chemical plant?

A. Better
B. Less Quality
C. Same
D. None
11.

D isomer of the drug isoproterenol, used to treat which disease?

A. Mild asthma
B. Heart disease
C. Diabetes
D. Obesity

12.

After a replication fork has been halted, it can be restored by at least two major paths, both of which require which protein?

A. RecA
B. RecB
C. RecC
D. RecD

13.

During transcription, an enzyme system converts the genetic information in a segment of double-stranded DNA into which strand?

A. RNA
B. DNA
C. Plasmid
D. Nucleus

14.

Unlike DNA polymerase, RNA polymerase does not require what to initiate synthesis?

A. Gene

B. Primer
C. Strand
D. Nucleotide

15.

The DNA-dependent RNA polymerase of E. coli is a large, complex enzyme with how many core subunits?

A. Six
B. Five
C. Four
D. Three

16.

The error rate for transcription is how much as compared to that for chromosomal DNA replication?

A. Lower
B. Higher
C. Medium
D. Lesser

17.

Many RNA polymerases, including bacterial RNA polymerase and the eukaryotic RNA polymerase II what they do when a mispaired base is added during transcription?

A. Speed
B. Slower
C. Pause
D. Fast Reversed

18.

Protein binding can do what during transcription by facilitating either RNA polymerase binding or steps further along in the initiation process?

A. Deactivate
B. Activate
C. Lined up
D. None
19.

The principal function of RNA polymerase II (Pol II) is synthesis of which RNA out of following?

A. rRNAs
B. mRNAs
C. tRNAs
D. None
20.

Pol II is a huge enzyme with how many subunits?

A. 15
B. 13
C. 12
D. 11
21.

Rifampicin inhibits which bacterial synthesis?

A. RNA
B. DNA
C. Proteins
D. Cytosol

22.

Amanita phalloides is name of which of following?

A. Fungus
B. Mushroom
C. Algae
D. Plants

23.

Certain segments of a protein sequence may be found in the organisms of one taxonomic group but not in other groups; these segments can be used as which type of sequences?

A. Non-Coding
B. Coding
C. Signature
D. Non-Specific

24.

Insertion of 12 amino acids near the amino terminus of the EF1α/EF-Tu proteins in all archaebacteria and eukaryotes but not in other types of bacteria, is an example of which of following?

A. Non-Coding Sequences
B. Coding Sequences
C. Signature Sequences
D. Non-Specific Sequences

25.

About how much energy in kJ/mol are required to break a single covalent bond?

A. 100-160 kJ/mol
B. 200-460 kJ/mol
C. 300-360 kJ/mol
D. 400-560 kJ/mol

26.

The fundamental unit of information in the living system is which out of following?

A. DNA
B. Chromosome
C. Gene
D. Plasmid

27.

RNA to Protein formation is termed as what?

A. Transduction
B. Translation
C. Transition
D. Transformation

28.

Small genomes of the yeast *Saccharomyces cerevisiae* have hoe many chromosomes?

A. 12
B. 16
C. 18
D. 20

29.

Human chromosomes range for the base pairs is up to which of the following?

A. 379 million bp
B. 59 million bp
C. 279 million bp
D. 89 million bp

30.

A portion of a chromosome that determines or affects a single character or which term for a visible property, such as eye colour?

A. Genotype
B. Phenotype
C. Monotype
D. Serotype

31.

George Beadle and Edward Tatum proposed a molecular definition of which of following in 1940?

A. DNA
B. RNA
C. Gene
D. Chromosome

32.

Which genetic defect in phytanoyl-CoA hydroxylase, leads to very high blood levels of phytanic acid and severe neurological problems including blindness and deafness?

A. Refsum's disease
B. Motor Neuron Disease
C. Gullian Barr Syndrome
D. Rheumatic fever

33.

People with genetic defects in any enzyme involved in urea formation cannot tolerate diets rich in which nutrient?

A. Fats
B. Protein
C. Carbohydrates
D. Minerals

34.

Melanin synthesis from tyrosine is defective in which disease out of following?

A. Albinism
B. Argenimia
C. Alkeptonuria
D. Homocystienuria

35.

Methylmalonic acidemia (MMA) a recessive genetic disorder of amino acid metabolism, MMA has symptoms almost identical with those caused by which disease?

A. ethylene glycol poisoning
B. Ascorbic acid poisoning
C. Arsenic Poisoning
D. Heavy metals toxicity

36.

In the maple syrup urine disease, which acid accumulated in blood and "Spill Over" in urine?

A. 3 branched α-keto acid
B. 2 branched α-amino acid
C. Hydrochloric Acid
D. Sulphuric Acid

37.

Cytochrome P-450 is a type of which type of protein?

A. Sulpha
B. Heme
C. Phosphorus
D. Nitrous

38.

Familial hypercholesterolemia, is a type of Human Disorder?

A. Acquired
B. Genetic
C. Contagious
D. Communicable

39.

Individuals having Familial hypercholesterolemia have a defective LDL receptor and lack receptor-mediated uptake of cholesterol carried by which of following?

A. HDL
B. VLDL

C. LDL

D. Triglyceride

40.

Lovastatin and compactin, are used to treat patients with familial hypercholesterolemia extracted from which of following?

A. Bacteria

B. Fungi

C. Viruses

D. Moulds

41.

In familial HDL deficiency, HDL levels are of which of following?

A. High

B. Very low

C. Very High

D. Normal

42.

Familial hypercholesterolemia and familial HDL deficiency genetic disorders are the result of mutations in which of the following?

A. Enzymes

B. ABC1 protein

C. Amylase 1

D. ARC 2 protein

43.

Adenosine deaminase (ADA) deficiency is an example of which of following?

A. Genetic aberrations in human pyrimidine metabolism
B. Genetic aberrations in human purine metabolism
C. Genetic aberrations in human nucleotide metabolism
D. Genetic aberrations in human cellular metabolism

44.

Beadle and Tatum concluded that a gene is a segment of genetic material that determines or codes for which of the following?

A. one enzyme
B. two enzymes
C. three enzymes
D. four enzymes

45.

A single E. coli cell contains almost how many times as much DNA as a bacteriophage λ particle?

A. 200
B. 100
C. 300
D. 150

46.

A yeast cell, one of the simplest eukaryotes, has how many times more DNA in its genome than an *E. coli* cell?

A. 4

B. 2.6

C. 3.6

D. 4.6

47.

Human cells have almost how many times DNA content as compared to *E.coli* cells?

A. 300

B. 400

C. 700

D. 100

48.

In a few organisms (trypanosomes, for example) each mitochondrion contains thousands of copies of mtDNA, organized into a complex and interlinked matrix known by which name?

A. Blast

B. Kinetoplast

C. Plasmid

D. cDNA

49.

Chloroplast DNA (cpDNA) also exists in which shape?

A. as circular duplexes

B. as oval duplexes

C. as square triplexes

D. as triangular triplexes

50.

Non-translated DNA segments in genes are called intervening sequences or which name?

A. Protons
B. Introns
C. Exons
D. Mutons

1. A	2. A	3. C	4. B	5. C	6. A	7. A	8. A	9. A	10. A
11. A	12. A	13. A	14. B	15. B	16. B	17. C	18. B	19. B	20. C
21. A	22. B	23. C	24. C	25. B	26. C	27. B	28. B	29. C	30. B
31. C	32. A	33. B	34. A	35. A	36. A	37. B	38. B	39. C	40. B
41. C	42. B	43. B	44. A	45. B	46. B	47. C	48. B	49. A	50. B

ANSWERS OF CHAPTER 12

CHAPTER XIII

Biodiversity

1.

The theory of origin of life which depicts that life has no origin is falls under which theory?

A. Special Creation
B. Spontaneous Generation
C. Steady-State
D. Cosmozoan

2.

Mannitol is the stored which food from following options?

A. Chara
B. Porphyra
C. Fucus
D. Gracillaria

3.

Tiger is not a resident in which one of the following national park

A. Ranthamhbor
B. Sunderbans
C. Gir
D. Jim Corbett

4.

India has more than 50,000 genetically different strains of rice, and how many varieties of mango?

A. 1000
B. 2000
C. 3000
D. 4000

5.

Medicinal plant *Rauwolfia vomitoria* growing in which mountain Regions?

A. Himalayan ranges
B. Aravali Ranges
C. Sahyaadri Ranges
D. Satpuda Mountains

6.

Western Ghats has which species diversity more as compared to the Eastern Ghats?

A. aves
B. amphibian
C. reptiles
D. mammals

7.

According to the IUCN (2004), the total number of plant and animal species described so far is slightly more than which of following?

A. 3 million
B. 1.5 million

C. 2.5 million

D. 3.5 million

8.

A more conservative and scientifically sound estimate of species on the Earth made by Robert places the global species diversity at about which number out of following?

A. 10 million

B. 8 million

C. 7 million

D. 11 million

9.

More than 70 per cent of all the species recorded are which of the following?

A. Animals

B. Plants

C. Fungi

D. Aquatic plants

10.

Plants comprise no more than which per cent of the total species?

A. 11

B. 22

C. 33

D. 44

11.

Among animals, insects are the most species-rich taxonomic group, making up more than which per cent of the total animals?

A. 90

B. 70

C. 60

D. 50

12.

India has only which per cent of the world's land area?

A. 4

B. 5

C. 2.4

D. 4.4

13.

How much percentage is the India's share of the global species diversity?

A. 8.1

B. 7.1

C. 9.1

D. 10.1

14.

India stands in first how many top mega diversity countries of the world?

A. 15

B. 14

C. 13

D. 12

15.

In general, species diversity ___________as we move away from the equator towards the poles.

A. Increases
B. Decreases
C. No change
D. Sometimes increase than decrease

16.

The largely tropical Amazonian rain forest in South America has which type of biodiversity on earth?

A. Smallest
B. Greatest
C. Medium
D. Discrete

17.

The IUCN Red List (2004) documents the extinction of how many species?

A. 800
B. 784
C. 984
D. 684

18.

The famous treaty on Biological Diversity signed by 150 countries on 5th June 1992 was held in which city?

A. Geneva
B. Washington
C. New Delhi
D. Rio de Janeiro
19.

As of 1990, how many genera of dinosaurs were estimated to ever have lived?

A. 900–1200
B. 600-700
C. 300-400
D. 100-200
20.

About 95% of all fossil species are which animals?

A. Terrestrial
B. Marine
C. Amphibian
D. Microorganisms
21.

Broadly 85% of today's recorded plants and animals are which type of following?

A. Terrestrial
B. Marine
C. Amphibian
D. Microorganisms
22.

Which of the following is the most abundant Green House Gas (GHG) in the earth's atmosphere?
A. Nitrogen Dioxide
B. Carbon Dioxide
C. Water Vapour
D. Sulphur Dioxide

23.

Veld type grasslands are located in which of following?
A. South Africa
B. South America
C. Australia
D. Britain

24.

Which one of the following is not included under In-situ conservation?
A. National Park
B. Botanical Gardens
C. Wild Life Sanctuary
D. Biosphere Reserve

25.

Which national park is famous for having Great Indian one Horned Rhino?
A. Raja ji National Park
B. Jim Corbet National Park
C. Bandipur National Park
D. Kajiranga National Park

26.

Which of the following region is a native place of the species of Yak (ox) and the Bharal?

   A. Uttarakhand
   B. Himachal Pradesh
   C. Tamilnadu
   D. Ladakh

27.

Which of the following is the natural habitat of the Indian lion?

A. Gir forest
B. Sunderban delta
C. Okhla Park
D. None of the above

28.

Which among the following is the World's largest Wetland System?

A. Camargue (France)
B. Okavango (Botswana)
C. Everglades (USA)
D. Pantanal (South America)

29.

Which of the following Environmentalists first gave the concept of Biodiversity 'hotspots'?

A. Gaylord Nelson
B. Norman Myers
C. John Muir
D. Jul

30.

All species of 'Lemur' are endemic to which among the following places of the world?

A. Seychelles Islands
B. Galapagos Islands
C. New Caledonia
D. Madagascar

31.

Which among the following terms of utmost significance in the dynamics of resource management was coined in the 'Brundtland Commission Report'?

A. Polluter-Pays Principle
B. Sustainable development
C. Inclusive Growth
D. Carrying Capacity

32.

With which of the following, the Agenda 21' of Rio Summit, 1992 is related to?

A. Sustainable development
B. Combating the consequences of population explosion.
C. Mitigation norms of Green House Gases (GHGs) emission.
D. Technology transfer mechanism to de

33.

Which among the following multilateral convention seeks to protect the human health and environment from Persistent Organic Pollutants (POPs)?

A. Bonn Convention
B. Stockholm Convention
C. Rotterdam Convention
D. Basel Convention

34.

The 'Montreaux Record' is a register of:

A. Invasive Alien Species and their ecological hazards outside their native environment.
B. Wetland sites under the threat of anthropogenic activities.
C. Endangered species of tropical and sub-tropical fauna
D. Coastal cities under direct threat of consequences of global warming.

35.

Which among the following chronic lung disease commonly known as 'black lung' disease, leads to reduced life expectancy in coal-miners?

A. Pneumoconiosis
B. Progressive Massive Fibrosis
C. Mesothelioma
D. Collier's Asthma

36.

Which among the following awards instituted by the Government of India for individuals or communities from rural areas that have shown extraordinary courage and dedication in protecting wildlife?

A. Indira Gandhi Paryavaran Puraskar

B. Medini Puruskar Yojana
C. Amrita Devi Bishnoi Award
D. Pitambar Pant National Award

37.

Which among the following is key faunal species that is being conserved and monitored in 'Dachigam National Park'?

A. Musk Deer
B. Golden Oriole
C. Yellow Throated Marten
D. Hangul or Kashmir Stag

38.

The 'thickness' of Stratospheric Ozone layer is measured in/on:

A. Sieverts
B. Dobson units
C. Melson units
D. Beaufort Scale

39.

Which among the following is the most abundant Green-House-Gas(GHG) in the earth's atmosphere? **(repeted question)**

A. Carbon dioxide
B. Water Vapour
C. Sulphur Dioxide
D. Tropospheric Ozone

40.

The Cartagena Protocol is regarding safe use, transfer and handling of:

A. Nuclear waste
B. Invasive Alien Species
C. Living Modified Organisms(LMO)
D. Toxic bye-products and industrial effluents

41.

The Western Ghats Ecology Expert Panel (WGEEP) is headed by:

A. R.K.Pachauri
B. Vandana Shiva
C. Madhav Gadgil
D. Pradip Krishen

42.

'Lion-tailed macaque' is the key faunal species of which Biosphere Reserve?

A. Nilgiri
B. Dehang-Debang
C. Dibru-Saikhowa
D. Nokrek

43.

An aquatic plant introduced from America to check pollution turned out to be a troublesome weed in Indian water bodies. The name of this 'invasive alien species is:

A. Opuntia
B. Aegilops

C. Eichhornia

D. Pistia

44.

In Nitrogen Cycle, soil nitrates are transformed into free nitrogen by:

A. Nitrifying bacteria

B. Denitrifying bacteria

C. Ammonifying bacteria

D. Both A and C

45.

Which one of the following is a useful biological indicator of Sulphur-dioxide pollution ?

A. Bryophytes

B. Algal blooms

C. Pseudomonas

D. Lichens

46.

The relationship between water fern Azolla and cyanobacterium Anabaena is :

A. Symbiotic

B. Mutualistic

C. Commensalism

D. Proto-Cooperation

47.

Which among the following always decreases in a Food chain across tropic levels?

A. Number
B. Accumulated chemicals
C. Energy
D. None of the above

48.

In the E-waste generated by the Mobile Phones, which among the following metal is most abundant?

A. Copper
B. Silver
C. Palladium
D. Gold

49.

Which among the following planet / body shows anti-greenhouse effect?

A. Mars
B. Venus
C. Jupiter
D. Titan

50.

In which of the following food chains, the Pyramid of Numbers will be always inverted?

A. Grassland Food chain
B. Ponds Food chain
C. Forests Food
D. Parasitic food chain

1. C	2. C	3. C	4. A	5. A	6. B	7. B	8. C	9. A	10. B
11. B	12. C	13. A	14. D	15. B	16. B	17. B	18. D	19. A	20. B
21. A	22. C	23. A	24. B	25. D	26. D	27. A	28. D	29. B	30. D
31. B	32. A	33. B	34. B	35. A	36. C	37. D	38. B	39. A	40. C
41. C	42. A	43. C	44. C	45. D	46. A	47. C	48. A	49. D	50. D

ANSWERS OF CHAPTER 13

CHAPTER XIV

Cellular Biology

1.

Glycolysis takes place in which part of cells?
A. Cell Wall
B. Nucleus
C. Cytosol
D. Golgi Bodies
2.

Embden, a German Chemist worked on which of following?
A. Krebs Cycle
B. Gluconeogenesis
C. Glycolysis
D. Electron Transport Chain
3.

The muscle phosphofructokinase is most complex emzyme it's basically what out of following in Yeasts ?
A. Tetramer
B. Monomer
C. Trimer
D. Octomer
4.

Rotenone, an inhibitor of Electron Transport Chain extracted from which part of plants?
A. Root
B. Stem
C. Leaves

D. Flowers

5.

Rotenone is ....to mammals
A. Most toxic
B. Less Toxic
C. Neutral
D. Beneficial

6.

Rutamycine is an antibiotic which can supress which out of following?
A. Electron Transport Chain
B. Oxidative Phosphorylation
C. Both A and B
D. None of above

7.

Hexokinase found in all tissues and exists in how many forms?
A. 2
B. 3
C. 4
D. 5

8.

Cells with nuclear envelopes are called as what?

A. Eukaryotes
B. Prokaryotes
C. Fungus
D. Bacteria

9.

Many organisms that have evolved in anaerobic environments are obligate anaerobes: they die when exposed to which gas?

A. Oxygen
B. Nitrogen
C. Carbon Dioxide
D. Carbon Mono-oxide

10.

Chemotrophs may be further classified as lithotrophs and which one out of following?

A. Organotrophs
B. Autotrophs
C. Heterotrophs
D. Anaerobic

11.

E. coli is a usually harmless inhabitant of which organ of human?

A. intestinal tract
B. Liver
C. Heart
D. Brain

12.

The cytoplasm (like that of most bacteria) contains one or smaller, circular segments of DNA called as what?

A. Genes
B. Viruses
C. Polymerase

D. Plasmids

13.

In which technique, cells or tissues in solution are disrupted by gentle homogenization?

A. Cell fractionation
B. Centrifuge
C. Chromatography
D. Spectrophotometry

14.

Electron microscopy reveals several types of protein filaments crisscrossing the eukaryotic cell, forming an interlocking three-dimensional meshwork, called as what?

A. cytoskeleton
B. cytoplasm
C. chloroplasts
D. cell organelles

15.

There are three general types of cytoplasmic filaments—actin filaments, microtubules, and intermediate filaments differing in which parameter?

A. Length
B. Width
C. Volume
D. Mass

16.

Exocytosis and endocytosis, are mechanisms of which of the following?

A. Locomotion
B. Respiration
C. Transport
D. Reproduction

17.

The monomeric subunits in proteins, nucleic acids, and polysaccharides are joined by which type of bonds?

A. Hydrogen
B. Covalent
C. Hydrophobic
D. Ionic

18.

Dissolved in the aqueous phase (cytosol) of all cells is a collection of how many different small organic molecules?

A. 100 to 200
B. 300 to 400
C. 500 to 600
D. 700 to 800

19.

If the system exchanges energy but not matter with its surroundings, it is a which type of system?

A. closed system
B. open system
C. semi closed system

D. semi open system

20.

Nearly all living organisms derive their energy, directly or indirectly, from the radiant energy of which source?

A. Moon
B. Sun
C. Earth
D. Mars

21.

The randomness or disorder of the components of a chemical system is expressed as what?

A. Entropy
B. Enthalpy
C. Thermodynamic
D. Heat

22.

The term "entropy," which literally means what?

A. "a change within"
B. "a change outside"
C. "a change all over"
D. None

23.

Cellular catalysts are, with a few exceptions, of which type?

A. Carbohydrates

B. Proteins
C. Fats
D. Vitamins

24.

The term biochemistry was coined by which scientist?

A. Carl Neuberg
B. Boron Justus von Liebig
C. Friedrich Wohler
D. Karl Wilher Scheel

25.

DDT was considered as which generation pesticide?

A. Second
B. First
C. Third
D. Fourth

26.

Which is the unit of mutation?

A. Codon
B. Gene
C. Muton
D. Proton

27.

What is name of longest single celled organism?

A. *Caulerpa taxifolia*
B. *Pheonix dactylefera*

C. *Thermoccocus aqaticus*

D. *Paramacium*

28.

Out of following which is non-nucleated cell of plants?

A. Parenchyma

B. Plastids

C. Sieve tubes

D. Chloroplasts

29.

Which fungus/fungi is/are responsible for wart disease in potatoes?

A. Synchytrium

B. Plasmodiphore

C. Both A and B

D. None

30.

Cellulose has how much tensile strength?

A. Low

B. High

C. Moderate

D. None

31.

Out of following which is acidic sugar?

A. Rhamnose

B. Galactose

C. Galactouronic sugar

D. Arbinose

32.

Presence of Ca^{2+} and Mg^{2+} ions makes pectin which type out of following?

A. Solid

B. Gel

C. Liquid

D. Powder

33.

Enzymes typically show maximal catalytic activity at a characteristic pH, called what?

A. pH optimum

B. pH acidic

C. pH alkaline

D. pH neutral

34.

A mixture of a weak acid (or base) and its salt resists changes in pH caused by the addition of H^+ or OH^-. The mixture thus functions as what?

A. Acid

B. Buffer

C. Alkali

D. Solvent

35.

Lignification is characteristics of which type of tissues/ Cells?

A. Animal tissues
B. Plant tissues
C. Bacterial Cells
D. Spores

36.

Out of following, which is an indication of transition between aquatic habitats to terrestrial habitat?

A. Acidification
B. Lignification
C. Alkalization
D. Bone formation

37.

Suberin, is chemically which type of compound?

A. Carbohydrates
B. Fats
C. Vitamins
D. Minerals

38.

Suberization occurs in which type of cells?

A. Cork and endodermis
B. Spores and Bacteria
C. Viruses
D. Hepatic Cells

39.

The process of thickening of cells wall due to deposition of permanent cell wall materials below the first line of wall is termed as what?

A. Aposition
B. Thickening
C. Softening
D. Thinning

40.

What is the name of process of thickening of cell wall due to deposition of permanent wall material between particles of first wall spaces?

A. Aposition
B. Intussusception
C. Thickening
D. Thinning

41.

What is name of the intercellular transportation of solutes through plasmodesmata?

A. Symplastic Transport
B. Passive Transport
C. Active Transport
D. Tubular Transport

42.

In which year the famous fluid mosaic model was proposed by S J Singer and G L Nicolson?

A. 1965

B. 1972

C. 1980

D. 1985

43.

Integral Membrane properties of the cell membrane can be grouped into how many categories?

A. 3

B. 4

C. 2

D. 5

44.

Glycoproteins and Glycolipids collectively form which of following?

A. Glycocalyx

B. Glycolysis

C. Glucose

D. Glucagon

45.

Out of following options what is tendency of membrane to become fluid at high temperature?

A. More

B. Less

C. Moderate

D. Very Less

46.

Out of 3 classes of lipids in plasma membrane is Glycerophospholipids, Steroids and which one more?

A. Triglycerides
B. Cholesterol
C. Sphingophospholipids
D. Phosphates

47.

Which compound out of following is present in the ABO blood group antigens?

A. Glycolipids
B. Glucose
C. Glycoproteins
D. Fats

48.

The heat capacity of water is the amount of heat required to raise the temperature of how much kg of water by 1°C?

A. 1 Kg
B. 10 Kg
C. 100 Kg
D. 1000 Kg

49.

Ribose, deoxyribose and ribulose are which type of carbohydrate out of following?

A. Hexose
B. Pentose

C. Triose

D. Mannose

50.

When starch is digested by Amylase which product formed out of following?

A. Lactose

B. Sucrose

C. Maltose

D. Mannose

1. C	2. C	3. A	4. A	5. B	6. C	7. D	8. A	9. A	10. A
11. A	12. D	13. A	14. A	15. B	16. C	17. B	18. A	19. A	20. B
21. A	22. A	23. B	24. A	25. B	26. C	27. A	28. C	29. C	30. B
31. C	32. B	33. A	34. B	35. B	36. B	37. B	38. A	39. A	40. B
41. A	42. B	43. B	44. A	45. A	46. C	47. A	48. A	49. B	50. C

ANSWERS OF CHAPTER 14

Refrences

1. Anatomy & Physiology, Volume 3,ISBN 978-1-304-84331-9,textbook equity edition,2013
2. Basics of Bioinformatics, Rui Jiang Xuegong Zhang Michael Q. Zhang Editors,Lecture Notes of the Graduate Summer School on Bioinformatics of China, ISBN 978-3-642-38951-1, 2013, Tsinghua university press and springer
3. Biochemistry and Human Nutrition by Rajiv Kapila, Animal Biochemistry Division, NDRI, Karnal, agreemoojn.com accessed on 03-04-2020.
4. Biophysics, Vasantha Pattabhi N. Gautham Department of Crystallography & Biophysics University of Madras, Guindy Campus Chennai, India, KLUWER ACADEMIC PUBLISHERS NEW YORK,
5. BOSTON, DORDRECHT, LONDON, MOSCOW, Narosa Publishing House DELHI CHENNAI MUMBAI KOLKATA, eBook ISBN: 0-306-47520-0 Print ISBN: 1-4020-0218-1,2002
6. Biophysics, Vasantha Pattabhi N. Gautham, Kluwer Academic Publishers New York,Boston, Dordrecht,London,Moscow,2002
7. Biotechnology, John E Smith, University of Strathclyde, Cambridge University Press, ISBN 978-0-511-46394-5, 1981, 1988, 2009
8. https://www.antibodies-online.com/resources/17/1215/radioimmunoassay-ria/accessed on 08-02-2020
9. https://www.indiabix.com/biochemistry/tca-cycle/034005
10. https://www.shodex.com/en/kouza/

a.html#!accessed on 08-20-2020

11. https://www.studyandscore.com/studymaterial-detail/flame-photometer-principle-components-working-procedure-applications-advantages-and-disadvantages/accessed on 08-02-2020

12. Lehninger Principle of Biochemistry, fourth edition, David L. Nelson and Michael M Cox, www.whfreeman.com/lehninger4e, 0-7167-5952-7,accessed in January 2020.

13. Nurse's Manual of Laboratory and Diagnostic Tests, Edition 4, Bonita Morrow Cavanaugh, PhD, F.A. Davis Company • Philadelphia,2003

Disclaimer

I made all Questions carefullly and tried to avaoid errros. But if any error occured due to haman errors for that I offer deep apology from readers. Your comments on book are welcome, so write me at snarwadiya@gmail.com. The book hope will fullfill your objective and you will gain something new knowledge from the book.

www.ingramcontent.com/pod-product-compliance
Lightning Source LLC
Chambersburg PA
CBHW071246150726
48001CB00018B/156